God Bless America

Scriptures, Devotions & Prayers
★ ★ ★ ★ *for Our Nation* ★ ★ ★ ★

GOD BLESS AMERICA

Scriptures, Devotions & Prayers

★★★★ *for Our Nation* ★★★★

BONNIE RICKNER JENSEN

A 60-DAY DEVOTIONAL

PARACLETE
PRESS
BREWSTER, MASSACHUSETTS

2026 First Printing

God Bless America: Scriptures, Devotions & Prayers for Our Nation, A 60-Day Devotional

ISBN 979-8-89348-050-4

Library of Congress Control Number: 2025948268

10 9 8 7 6 5 4 3 2 1

Published by Paraclete Press
Brewster, Massachusetts
www.paracletepress.com

Printed in South Korea

CONTENTS

The LORD has made known His salvation;
His righteousness He has revealed
in the sight of the nations.

—PSALM 98:2

DAY 1

LOVE

Almighty God, we make our earnest prayer that
Thou wilt incline the hearts of the citizens
To cultivate a spirit of subordination and
Obedience to government; to entertain a
Brotherly affection and love for one another and
For their fellow citizens of the United States at large.

—GEORGE WASHINGTON, FOUNDING FATHER
AND FIRST U.S. PRESIDENT, 1783

If God held a megaphone over our country today, His voice cheering us on toward love and unity would ring loudest. These two words hold the power to establish patience, civility, and peace. When we forgive one another, there is love. When we follow the Holy Spirit, there is unity. The apostle Paul understood the value of freedom, the importance of unity, and the power of love. He said, "I, therefore, the prisoner of the Lord, beseech you to walk worthy of the calling with which you were called, with all lowliness and gentleness, with longsuffering, bearing with one another in love, endeavoring to keep the unity of the Spirit in the bond of peace" (Ephesians 4:1–3).

Growing a powerful nation as a dwelling place for God starts with our dependence on the Holy Spirit to carry out God's command to *love one another*. If we don't rest assured in the power of love to save us, we risk being torn apart by division, dissension, and hatred. We unleash the fury of everything standing in opposition to the Father's perfect love. Love can steady us in the throes of any storm, the depths of any trial, and the winds of every change. Love suffers long and rejoices in truth; love *never* fails.

The most important commandments were given to us by the One who gave His life for us: Jesus said, " 'You shall love the Lord your God with all your heart, with all your soul, and with all your mind.' This is the first and great commandment. And the second is like it: 'You shall love your neighbor as yourself' " (Matthew 22:37–39). Every blessing we hope to see hangs on our willing surrender to these two commands.

Now it shall come to pass, if you diligently obey the voice of the LORD your God, to observe carefully all His commandments . . . that the LORD your God will set you high above all nations of the earth. And all these blessings shall come upon you and overtake you, because you obey the voice of the LORD your God.

—DEUTERONOMY 28:1–2

REFLECT

In what ways can you consistently reflect the love of God to others?

In what way will you intentionally nurture an environment of love and service in your neighborhood or community this week?

In self-reflection, describe what attributes of love you would ask God to help you put into practice.

PRAY

Father, show me the ways I can make Your love my priority today—through service to others, the sacrifice of my own comfort, and the fullness of Your compassion, especially toward those with whom I may not agree. Amen.

DAY 2

PATRIOT

These are the times that try men's souls. The summer soldier and the sunshine patriot will, in this crisis, shrink from the service of their country; but he who stands by it now, deserves the love and thanks of man and woman. Tyranny, like hell, is not easily conquered; yet we have this consolation with us, that the harder the conflict, the more glorious the triumph.

—THOMAS PAINE, AMERICAN REVOLUTION AUTHOR,
THE AMERICAN CRISIS NO. 1, 1776

From its inception and by the mercy of God, our nation has sustained a determination to stand in the face of every adversity. Consequently, in God's hand alone we rest secure. "For the LORD is the great God, and the great King above all gods. In His hand are the deep places of the earth; the heights of the hills are His also. The sea is His, for He made it; and His hands formed the dry land" (Psalm 95:3–5).

In 1776, Thomas Paine experienced the fortitude of the colonies waning beneath the pressures of the Revolutionary War. Our burgeoning country could not know how long or perilous the fight would be, but God knew. The conflict stretched from 1775 to 1783, when the chains of tyranny were finally broken. Free and united, the USA began its journey as a liberated people. Thirteen colonies strong at the time, our country was defined by patriots who defended it at all costs—believing the unalienable rights of life, liberty, and the pursuit of happiness were endowed by our Creator. "For you who fear my name, the Sun of Righteousness will rise with healing in his wings. And you will go free, leaping with joy like calves let out to pasture" (Malachi 4:2, TLB).

The defense of freedom is not easy, the foundation of truth is not easily laid, and the path of a great nation is not one of ease. Still today, we celebrate what we have endured—through sorrow, sacrifice, and the sovereignty of God—with a hope held fast by His unfailing love.

Declare His glory among the nations,
His wonders among all peoples.
For the LORD is great and greatly to be praised.

—1 CHRONICLES 16:24–25

REFLECT

If you could speak to a patriot from the time of the Revolutionary War, what would you tell them makes you most proud of our country today?

What gives you hope for America's future?

How would you define the pursuit of happiness in a contemporary way, and in what ways is your relationship with God a key factor?

PRAY

Father, I lift our country into the hands of Your mercy. I ask You to move through the hearts of those who love and serve You, to cultivate a spirit of unity, kindness, and peace. Amen.

DAY 3

FREEDOM

O say can you see, by the dawn's early light
What so proudly we hail'd at the twilight's last gleaming
Whose broad stripes and bright stars through the perilous fight
O'er the ramparts we watch'd, were so gallantly streaming?
And the rocket's red glare, the bombs bursting in air
Gave proof through the night that our flag was still there;
O say does that star-spangled banner yet wave
O'er the land of the free and the home of the brave?

—"THE STAR-SPANGLED BANNER,"
FIRST VERSE, FRANCIS SCOTT KEY, 1814

When the light of a new day washed over Fort McHenry on the morning of September 14, 1814, the stars and stripes became the symbol of an infant nation in the hands of an eternal God. Francis Scott Key felt compelled to capture the emotion he felt when he witnessed the Great Garrison Flag flying over the Baltimore fort following a relentless British attack. The land of the free and the home of the brave saw God move a nation forward against all odds.

Freedom is a gift from God. The greatest gift is our release from the bondage of sin through the sacrifice of Jesus Christ. Every day we have the privilege of waking up in a land unburdened by the fear of *freely* serving our Heavenly Father and worshiping our victorious Savior. The sunrise brings with it endless mercies and countless reasons to thank God for the country He's given us. We enjoy the beauty of our freedom by the power He has bestowed.

God told Abraham, "In your seed all the nations of the earth shall be blessed, because you have obeyed My voice" (Genesis 22:18). God's voice still speaks to those who will listen, and obedience is still the path to blessing. The goodness of God flows through all leaders who serve Him and follow His will with humble hearts. Prayer is a path of surrender to God's wisdom and will for our great country. We move the heart of God by placing our hope in Him alone.

Stand fast therefore in the liberty by which Christ has made us free.

—GALATIANS 5:1

REFLECT

How does it make you feel to have the freedom to worship God every day?

In what ways do you stay mindful of freedoms in America and not take them for granted?

Make a list of freedoms you consider most important. How do you express your gratefulness to God?

PRAY

Father, make the hearts of our President and Vice President pliable for the shaping of Your will. Give each a teachable spirit and a desire to follow You every day, so the blessings of heaven flow freely to the great country You've allowed us to live in. Amen.

DAY 4

PILGRIM

My country 'tis of thee,
Sweet land of liberty,
Of thee I sing;
Land where my fathers died,
Land of the pilgrims' pride,
From every mountainside
Let freedom ring.

—"MY COUNTRY 'TIS OF THEE," FIRST VERSE,
SAMUEL FRANCES SMITH, 1831

Every blessing on earth comes through the sovereignty of heaven. Every country that rises does so under the watchful eye of our mighty God. We're modern-day pilgrims traveling through this world en route to our eternal home. The nineteenth-century preacher Charles Spurgeon wrote, "I am a pilgrim in the world, but at home in my God. I wander, but in God I dwell in quiet habitation." Serving God is the way to a soul at peace while we're here, even through the most difficult times and trials that are beyond our reasoning. His love will carry us without fail.

The pilgrims who came to America in 1620 were seeking liberty to serve God according to His word, loosed from any other framework or guiding principle. Over two hundred years later on July 4, 1831, the patriotic hymn "My Country 'Tis of Thee" was performed by a children's choir in Boston. The inspired words written by Samuel F. Smith served as our unofficial national anthem until the adoption of "The Star-Spangled Banner" in 1931.

God has His way in the life of our nation in the same way He has His way in our individual lives—through a constant willingness to trust and obey Him. Each day we have the opportunity to echo the words of the psalmist, "For these laws of yours have been my source of joy and singing through all these years of my earthly pilgrimage. I obey them even at night and keep my thoughts, O Lord, on you. What a blessing it has been to me—to constantly obey" (Psalm 119:54–56, TLB).

Sing to the LORD, all the earth;
Proclaim the good news of His salvation
from day to day.

—1 CHRONICLES 16:23

REFLECT

What daily acts of obedience in your life honor God and bless our country?

With a mindset of pilgrimage through this earthly existence, how do you sow seeds for future generations?

How will you put God first today?

PRAY

Father, give our government officials the desire to obey Your word and be a light to the nations around the globe. Fill each of them with joy and strength as they follow You every day. Amen.

DAY 5

HERITAGE

Our country is in danger, but not to be despaired of. Our enemies are numerous and powerful; but we have many friends, determining to be free, and heaven and earth will aid the resolution. On you [US citizens] depend the fortunes of America. You are to decide the important question, on which rests the happiness and liberty of millions yet unborn. Act worthy of yourselves.

—DR. JOSEPH WARREN, FOUNDING FATHER, PHYSICIAN, AND PRESIDENT OF THE MASSACHUSETTS CONGRESS, 1775

It is God who controls the nations and deserves daily praise for the birth of the United States of America. Our hearts bow in humble adoration for His eternal majesty, divine protection, and guiding hand. Wisdom to lead comes from the desire to know God's Word and to understand how vital it is to follow God's commands. The spirit of our country finds its strength in the Spirit of God, and the heritage of this powerful nation rests on the divine determination of those who came before us.

Dr. Joseph Warren was regarded as an inspirational figure in colonial America. He often spoke to patriotic crowds, motivating them in their fight for freedom. He once prayed, "May we ever be a people favored of God." Dr. Warren's simple request can be echoed today as we navigate through a world influenced by dark spiritual forces. Our greatest enemy cannot be seen or met on a battlefield. Our weapons of victory are wielded in prayer and taking up the Armor of God.

> Use every piece of God's armor to resist the enemy whenever he attacks, and when it is all over, you will still be standing up.
>
> But to do this, you will need the strong belt of truth and the breastplate of God's approval. Wear shoes that are able to speed you on as you preach the Good News of peace with God. In every battle you will need faith as your shield to stop the fiery arrows aimed at you by Satan. And you will need the helmet of salvation and the sword of the Spirit—which is the Word of God (Ephesians 6:13–17, TLB).

Servants of the Savior inherit the blessings of God, the privilege of peace, and the hope of eternity. Be encouraged by these words from the Apostle John: "Grace to you and peace from Him who is and who was and who is to come . . . from Jesus Christ, the faithful witness, the firstborn from the dead, and the ruler over the kings of the earth" (Revelation 1:4–5).

"No weapon turned against you shall succeed, and you will have justice against every courtroom lie. This is the heritage of the servants of the Lord. This is the blessing I have given you," says the Lord.

—ISAIAH 54:17, TLB

REFLECT

In reading about the birth of our nation, how are you inspired to be more diligent in prayer for our country?

In what ways do you see the "favor of God" on America?

Do you feel spiritual battles are on the increase in our country? What Scriptures do you reference when praying against the principalities of darkness?

PRAY

Father, I pray for strength in You and the power of Your might. Give us faith and unity as a people, in spiritual support of our leaders, for the good of all citizens and the salvation of all groups of people. Amen.

DAY 6

LIBERTY

God who gave us life gave us liberty. And can the liberties of a nation be thought secure when we have removed their only firm basis, a conviction in the minds of people that these liberties are the gift of God? That they are not to be violated without His wrath? Indeed I tremble for my country when I reflect that God is just; that His justice cannot sleep forever.

—THOMAS JEFFERSON, FOUNDING FATHER AND THIRD U.S. PRESIDENT, 1781

God is the beginning of every good thing, the One who sustains the blessings we enjoy. His love is the hope that holds the power to unite us. Division fosters the lie that God has turned His back on us—if things don't go the way we believe they should, God is no longer in control. There is no deception more damaging to the unity of a nation.

King David expressed his praises to the Lord in the presence of the whole assembly when he said,

> Everything in the heavens and earth is yours, O Lord. . . . We adore you as being in control of everything. Riches and honor come from you alone, and you are the ruler of all mankind; your hand controls power and might, and it is at your discretion that men are made great and given strength. (1 Chronicles 29:11–12, TLB)

Thomas Jefferson understood the gifts of God. Life and liberty are priceless among them. President Jefferson saw the security of our nation threatened by the lack of that conviction in the minds of its people as early as the eighteenth century. There is no security outside of Jesus Christ, and there is no unity apart from God's love. We are bound by both if we are to correct our way forward.

Believing our lives *and* liberties are gifts from God remains the firm basis on which we stand. "Whatever is good and perfect comes to us from God, the Creator of all light, and he shines forever without change or shadow" (James 1:17, TLB).

Where the Spirit of the Lord is, there is liberty.

—2 CORINTHIANS 3:17

REFLECT

What good gifts are you most thankful for?

How can you remain anchored to the hope that God is in control of our nation?

When you're tempted to walk in judgment of those who disagree with you, what truths steer you toward God's love?

PRAY

Father, impress on my heart and on the hearts of those in my community that Your love and longsuffering are gifts we should offer one another. Build a spirit of unity in my neighborhood, in my city, in my state, and in this nation. Keep us from grieving Your Spirit. Amen.

DAY 7

GLORY

Mine eyes have seen the glory of the coming of the Lord;
He is trampling out the vintage where the grapes of wrath are stored;
He hath loosed the fateful lightning of His terrible swift sword;
His truth is marching on.

—"THE BATTLE HYMN OF THE REPUBLIC,"
FIRST VERSE, JULIA WARD HOWE, 1865

While our spirit exclaims the constant refrain, "*Glory, glory, hallelujah*," our hearts and minds battle the forces of darkness in this world with determination. The apostle Paul reminds us, "We also glory in tribulations, knowing that tribulation produces perseverance" (Romans 5:3). The hardships we go through produce the tenacity to make us, as one nation, a clearer reflection of *every* fruit the Spirit of God produces: love, joy, peace, long-suffering, kindness, goodness, faithfulness, gentleness, and self-control.

We are imperfect people in a broken world, and it will be no other way until Jesus returns. When a new day dawned on our divided nation in 1865, the lyric of *The Battle Hymn of the Republic* flowed through the pen of Julia Ward Howe. Even today, our spiritual eyes must remain open and ready for the coming of the Lord—and it should be the rejoicing of every heart. When perfect love reigns, war will end. When truth rules the nations, peace will be the eternal reward.

God is the hope of every good outcome we desire for our country. Following Him leads to love that prevails, no matter what we are faced with and what we must endure. As King David expressed in the presence of the assembly, "Yours, O Lord, is the greatness, The power and the glory, The victory and the majesty; For all that is in heaven and in earth is Yours" (1 Chronicles 29:11). God's absolute authority is where we can put both our hope *and* trust because His endless compassion will sustain us.

The time will come when all the earth is filled, as the waters fill the sea, with an awareness of the glory of the Lord.

—HABAKKUK 2:14, TLB

REFLECT

Why might it be hard for you to depend on God during times of suffering?

When our nation is divided, what steps do you think we can take to change it? We can ask God to help us put these Scriptures into practice—John 13:34–35; John 15:12, 17; Romans 12:10; Galatians 5:13.

How do you offer others the compassion you've experienced during a trial?

PRAY

Father, inspire us to love one another as You have loved us. I praise You for the strength of our ancestors through times of division and sorrow. May You see us through our tribulations with the same compassion. Amen.

OF LEV XXV V X PROCLAIM LIBERT
NE IN PHILADA BY ORDER OF THE AS
PASS & STOW
PHILADA
MDCCLIII

DAY 8

COURAGE

I have the most animating confidence that the present noble struggle for our liberty will terminate gloriously for America. And let us play the man for our God, and for the cities of our God; while we are using the means in our power, let us humbly commit our righteous cause to the great Lord of the Universe. . . .

—JOHN HANCOCK, MEMBER OF THE U.S. CONTINENTAL CONGRESS, 1774

From the inception of the United States of America, our nation's existence has done more to reveal the faithfulness of God than any human or earthly claim on its success. Our country wouldn't be here without God's intervention, and we would be foolish to forget it. The great men and women who courageously forged ahead in the face of every impossibility, through the peril of physical emaciation and inclement forces of nature, deserve the honor and gratefulness due them. But to separate the goodness of our magnificent God from the greatness of our blessed nation is to misdirect our highest praise from its rightful place.

The kind of bravery, selflessness, and sacrifice it took to build our nation came directly from heaven by the mercy of God. G. K. Chesterton wrote, "Courage is almost a contradiction in terms. It means a strong desire to live taking the form of a readiness to die." For over 200 years, we as a people have known the value of courage and the cost of bravery. And since the beginning of time, God has filled the hearts of humans with divine courage to overcome, often against impossible odds.

"Be strong and of good courage, do not fear nor be afraid of them; for the LORD your God, He is the One who goes with you. He will not leave you nor forsake you" (Deuteronomy 31:6). God is our hope in all of life's battles. Through every anxiety-ridden day and mountain-moving challenge, He *never* abandons us.

Be of good courage, and let us be strong for our people and for the cities of our God. And may the LORD do what is good in His sight.

—2 SAMUEL 10:12

REFLECT

How have you experienced God's presence and empowerment during your life?

In what ways do you feel we've moved away from God as a country?

What do you think are practical ways you can move yourself, your family, and your community toward a more God-fearing, grateful posture?

PRAY

Father, bring our country closer to You, beginning with my family. Let my actions and words bring honor and gratefulness to You. Let my love for You be evident and contagious to those around me. Amen.

DAY 9

LIGHT

Thus out of small beginnings greater things have been produced by His hand that made all things of nothing and gives being to all things that are; and as one small candle may light a thousand, so the light here kindled hath shone unto many, yea in some sort to our whole nation; let the glorious name of Jehovah have all praise.

—WILLIAM BRADFORD, FIRST GOVERNOR OF PLYMOUTH COLONY, 1620

In the broadening light of a new world, our founders gave all praise to the glorious name of Jehovah, the great I AM. "*Who has done such mighty deeds, directing the affairs of generations of mankind as they march by? It is I, the Lord, the First and Last; I alone am he*" (Isaiah 41:4, TLB, emphasis added). The Light of the World produces good; whatever is good and perfect comes from the heart of God.

William Bradford arranged the first Thanksgiving, long before President Abraham Lincoln issued a proclamation for the observance in 1863. The first settlers offered their gratefulness to God, where it belonged. "So we, Your people and the sheep of Your pasture, Will give You thanks forever; We will show forth Your praise to all generations" (Psalm 79:13). The pilgrims risked the dangers of the unknown and saw God "make all things from nothing." The settlers worked hard and witnessed, from meager and difficult beginnings, the grace of God unfold day by day. From sunrises over the Atlantic to sunsets following days of loss, suffering, and sacrifice, they trusted the sovereignty and strength of God to see them through.

Their tenacity became the kindling that would light a whole nation. The hardships they endured laid a foundation of humility beneath the benevolence of God. We are bound by the same conviction that all things come from the Creator's hand, and all our praise is due Him.

For you are the Fountain of life; our light is from your light. Pour out your unfailing love on those who know you! Never stop giving your blessings to those who long to do your will.

—PSALM 36:9–10, TLB

REFLECT

In what ways do you humble yourself before the Lord?

In what areas of your life has God revealed pride or ego and helped you overcome?

How is God using you to shine His light through your life and into the world?

PRAY

Father, open the eyes of our state and local leaders to the danger of pride and the gift of humility. Create in them clean hearts for Your glory and encourage each one of us to shine Your light in this nation. Amen.

DAY 10

DUTY

Our obligations to our country never cease but with our lives.

—JOHN ADAMS, FOUNDING FATHER AND
SECOND U.S. PRESIDENT, 1808

For citizens of this powerful nation, our hope for our leaders should be that they have a desire to mirror young Solomon's prayer as he became king:

> Here I am among your own chosen people, a nation so great that there are almost too many people to count! Give me an understanding mind so that I can govern your people well and know the difference between what is right and what is wrong. For who by himself is able to carry such a heavy responsibility?
> (1 Kings 3:8–10, TLB)

The duty of our leaders is a weighty one, and each assignment should encourage humility. Those in authority are in the service of God for the good of others, and their success depends on Him.

John Adams was a founding father who helped compose our Declaration of Independence and aided in early diplomacy with Europe. Duty and sacrifice were paramount in his thinking—an "obligation" for the people who called our developing nation home. It was God who moved the pieces into place to form a united people with a single hope to serve and worship Him freely. We owe our heavenly Father all our praise, for "He enlarges nations, and guides them" (Job 12:23).

The ultimate battle for the soul of our nation belongs to God, and to Him it can be wholeheartedly entrusted through prayer. We can find encouragement from the words of Joshua, who at a very old age shared with the leaders of Israel, "For the Lord your God is He who fights for you, as He promised you. Therefore take careful heed to yourselves, that you love the Lord your God" (Joshua 23:10b–11).

Here is my final conclusion: fear God and obey his commandments, for this is the entire duty of man.

—ECCLESIASTES 12:13, TLB

REFLECT

How might you make a habit of praying for those in authority?

What specific challenge in our country might you take to God in prayer for the next 30 days?

How can you lift up the spiritual health of our nation in thought, word, and deed?

PRAY

Father, renew a right spirit within our community leaders and those in authority over the education of our children. Let Your love be the greatest influence on teachers, librarians, principals, administrators, and superintendents. Give me wisdom to do all I can to express truth and love toward those instructing our children. Amen.

NATION
GOD
FOR IN
THEE
PUT MY
TRUST

DAY 11

RESILIENCE

Preserve me, O God: for in thee do I put my trust.

—PSALM 16:1 (KJV), INSCRIPTION WITHIN THE U.S. CAPITOL BUILDING PRAYER ROOM

There is truth engraved in the stained glass window of the U.S. Capitol Prayer Room. As light streams through its colorful panels, those who go there to pray, meditate, and be still are reminded to put their trust in God. Every prayer lifted from this nation should begin with gratitude for the sustaining strength God has provided over the years. Our nation's resilience is owed to His faithfulness. To think, in the slightest measure, that it's time for a more self-sufficient perspective as we press forward is to leave out the One who established us in the first place. "He rules by His power forever; His eyes observe the nations" (Psalm 66:7).

The window in this dedicated room depicts George Washington kneeling in prayer—a fitting reflection of the words he spoke in his first inaugural address. "It would be peculiarly improper to omit in this first official act, my fervent supplications to that Almighty Being who rules over the universe, who presides in the councils of the nations, and whose providential aids can supply every human defect, that His benediction may consecrate to the liberties and happiness of the people of the United States."

God indeed presides in the councils of the nations. "The eyes of the Lord are in every place, Keeping watch on the evil and the good" (Proverbs 15:3). God *absolutely* can be trusted. "The word of the Lord is proven; He is a shield to all who trust in Him" (2 Samuel 22:31). God is, and forever will be, the strength and resilience of the America He has preserved.

The eyes of the Lord run to and fro throughout the whole earth, to show Himself strong on behalf of those whose heart is loyal to Him.

—2 CHRONICLES 16:9

REFLECT

List three things you're thankful for when reflecting on the United States of America.

God is our strength as a nation to recover from tragedy and trial. How have you seen or experienced His compassion personally? How has this affected your trust in Him?

How have you allowed God to deepen your faith in spite of the increasing darkness in the world? List out Scriptures you cling to.

PRAY

Father, compel the hearts of those who work in the U.S. Capitol Building to use the prayer room designated for them to spend moments with You. Quiet their hearts and minds. Give them a renewed desire to serve and trust You. Amen.

DAY 12

WISDOM

Wisdom is the principal thing; therefore, get wisdom: and with all thy getting get understanding.

—PROVERBS 4:7 (KJV), INSCRIPTION ON THE CEILING OF THE GREAT HALL IN THE LIBRARY OF CONGRESS

As one people bound by a mutual longing for a kinder, gentler union, it behooves us to seek the One who established our country, and by wisdom, founded the earth. "And to man He said, 'Behold, the fear of the Lord, that is wisdom, And to depart from evil is understanding'" (Job 28:28). God's Word is the source of absolute truth and eternal wisdom. Knowing it is the path to knowing *Him*, the way to deepen our reverence of Him, and the reason we have a desire to pursue what is right in His eyes.

We can choose, by the free will He's given us, to pray for the wisdom, knowledge, and understanding that will steer our nation toward all that is good. When we depend on the Holy Spirit for the understanding of God's Word, we develop a deep-seated longing to depart from the things that break God's heart. We depart from *anything* in opposition to His love and truth.

The verse from Proverbs that is etched on the ceiling of the Great Hall within the Library of Congress in our nation's capital reminds us that wisdom is the *principal* thing. It is critical and essential. The light of the Word is the only way to expel the darkness that threatens to obscure the blessings we've received from heaven since our country was born. Wisdom, with the understanding of how to apply it for our greatest good, will lead us into God's best. "If any of you lacks wisdom, let him ask of God, who gives to all liberally and without reproach, and it will be given to him" (James 1:5).

The LORD by wisdom founded the earth;
By understanding He established the heavens.

—PROVERBS 3:19

REFLECT

How often do you ask God to open your heart and mind to His wisdom?

James 1:5 says, "If any of you lacks wisdom, let him ask of God, who gives to all liberally and without reproach, and it will be given to him." Write a brief prayer to ask for wisdom and listen for understanding.

We are transformed by the knowledge of God's Word. In what ways has the Bible changed you?

PRAY

Father, we thank You today for the presence of Your word in the buildings of our nation's capital. From Hebrews 4:12, we know your Word is living and active; let Your truth come alive in those who lead this nation. Give them divine wisdom and the desire to follow Your will. Amen.

DAY 13

REPENTANCE

Whereas when our own beloved country, once, by the blessing of God, united, prosperous, and happy, is now afflicted with faction and civil war, it is peculiarly fit for us to recognize the hand of God in this terrible visitation, and in sorrowful remembrance of our own faults and crimes as a nation and as individuals to humble ourselves before Him and to pray for His mercy.

—ABRAHAM LINCOLN, SIXTEENTH U.S. PRESIDENT, 1861

The imperfection of our human state is more of a danger to our well-being as a country than any outside force coming against us. Humanity fell to its greatest enemy in the Garden of Eden, and no person or nation has been beyond the cruelty of its reach since. We have seen events in our world so defiantly opposite of God's love and mercy that it begs us to look within, as individuals of a united people, to plead for God's forgiveness. "Repent therefore and be converted, that your sins may be blotted out, so that times of refreshing may come from the presence of the Lord" (Acts 3:19).

Where do we go to find the humility and courage to *continually* oppose our self-sufficient and godless nature? The high and lofty One who inhabits eternity, the Holy One, says this: "I live in that high and holy place where those with contrite, humble spirits dwell; and I refresh the humble and give new courage to those with repentant hearts" (Isaiah 57:15, TLB). To our heavenly Father—who is slow to anger, full of compassion, and abounding in mercy—is where we need to go.

Our prayers are heard, but they must be offered daily, with honest and open hearts. When President Lincoln set aside a Day of National Humiliation, Prayer, and Fasting more than 150 years ago, he did so "in sorrowful remembrance of our [nation's] faults and crimes." The conviction he felt is one we should feel *still*, as the Holy Spirit leads us to become a more holy, whole, and united nation.

If My people who are called by My name will humble themselves, and pray and seek My face, and turn from their wicked ways, then I will hear from heaven, and will forgive their sin and heal their land.

—2 CHRONICLES 7:14

REFLECT

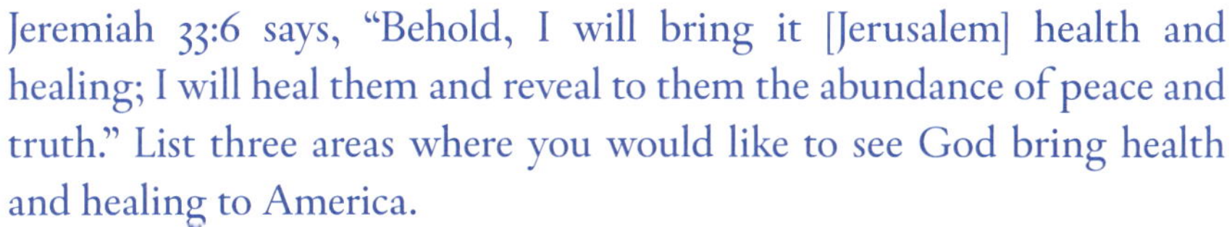

Jeremiah 33:6 says, “Behold, I will bring it [Jerusalem] health and healing; I will heal them and reveal to them the abundance of peace and truth.” List three areas where you would like to see God bring health and healing to America.

How has the Holy Spirit revealed ways for you to pray for humility and unity within your state?

Ask for God’s wisdom in how to pray for the leaders of your city.

PRAY

Father, thank You for the early leaders of this country who came to You with humble and repentant hearts and inspired us as a people to do the same. Give our current leaders a conviction to lead our communities into truth, transformation, and the righteousness of God in Christ Jesus. Amen.

IN GOD WE
TRUST

DAY 14

BRAVE

O thus be it ever when freemen shall stand
Between their lov'd home and the war's desolation!
Blest with vict'ry and peace, may the heav'n rescued land
Praise the power that hath made and preserv'd us as a nation!
Then conquer we must, when our cause it is just,
And this be our motto: "In God is our trust,"
And the star-spangled banner in triumph shall wave
O'er the land of the free and the home of the brave.

—"THE STAR-SPANGLED BANNER," FINAL VERSE,
FRANCIS SCOTT KEY, 1814

"Praise the power that hath made and preserv'd us as a nation!" To this little-known lyric of "The Star Spangled Banner," we offer a passionate *Amen!* The final verse of our national anthem then suggests this be our motto: *"In God is our trust."* Complete and unwavering trust in God is a decision. It's one we hope all of our leaders—from local, to state, to federal—make every day. In this world of brokenness, suffering, and constant trials, the bravery it takes to lead with divine intention and direction comes from God alone.

Prayerfully, we support those in authority, asking God to give them the courage to fight for His will to be done on earth as it is in heaven. "Wait for the Lord, and he will come and save you! Be brave, stouthearted, and courageous. Yes, wait and he will help you" (Psalm 27:14, TLB). Things will not always go the way we think they should or the way we want them to. But there is never a right time to question God's sovereignty. For the sake of strength and unity, we have to be brave enough to trust God implicitly. "The Lord is still in his holy temple; he still rules from heaven. He closely watches everything that happens here on earth" (Psalm 11:4, TLB).

When the author of our national anthem witnessed the miracle-working power of God in an early battle for the survival of our country, his words were inspired by the Author of our life's story. God knew our stories would find us here . . . in a nation free to serve and worship Him.

Watch, stand fast in the faith, be brave, be strong.

—1 CORINTHIANS 16:13

REFLECT

Who are the leaders you feel exhibit divine bravery when making decisions?

Each of us makes decisions all day, every day. How disciplined are you about praying for guidance from the Spirit of God?

How might God be prompting you to get more involved in leadership of any kind?

PRAY

Father, I put my trust in You to shape the hearts of our leaders. Today I ask you to strengthen the judges, prosecutors, district attorneys, public defenders, and all those in our judicial system to be brave as they stand for truth and what is right for our country. May Your Word be their light and justice be their guide. Amen.

DAY 15

DEVOTION

Laus Deo, meaning "Praise be to God."

—INSCRIPTION UPON THE ALUMINUM CAPSTONE AT THE TOP OF THE WASHINGTON MONUMENT, WASHINGTON DC'S TALLEST STRUCTURE

The tallest structure in our nation's capital, built by man and pointing to heaven, is inscribed *Laus Deo*, words that encapsulate the reason our nation exists: *Praise be to God.* These words face the rising sun. From the Pilgrims' arrival in 1620 to the vastness of our present home, God's innumerable gifts can be traced and remembered. He has been our strength, our refuge, our wisdom, our healing, and our hope. "All the nations—and you made each one—will come and bow before you, Lord, and praise your great and holy name" (Psalm 86:9, TLB).

In 1772, Samuel Adams wrote, "The right to freedom being the gift of the Almighty . . . The rights of the colonists as Christians . . . may be best understood by reading and carefully studying the institution of the Great Law Giver and Head of the Christian Church, which are to be found clearly written and promulgated in the New Testament." With glory for daily mercies due the Father, gratefulness for the gift of salvation due His Son, and gladness for divine power due the Holy Spirit, the New Testament remains our most valuable study guide. We won't have true success as a nation without heeding the examples set before us within the pages of God's Word.

A solemn and spiritual duty is to lift up political leaders in our daily conversations with God. By His grace we remain standing, and we are beholden to His faithfulness. May our hearts have a renewed devotion to lifting our nation to God, in praise for all He's done and all He will do as we honor Him.

May the God of peace himself make you entirely pure and devoted to God; and may your spirit and soul and body be kept strong and blameless until that day when our Lord Jesus Christ comes back again.

—1 THESSALONIANS 5:23, TLB

REFLECT

When considering the spiritual disciplines of prayer, fasting, and service, what are you most devoted to?

How do you follow the Apostle Paul's encouragement to "pray without ceasing" (1 Thessalonians 5:17)?

Do you make time daily to offer thankfulness and/or praise to God? How does it affect your day when you do or don't?

PRAY

Father, I thank You for the devotion and commitment of our first responders. I ask You to give them wisdom and discernment for every emergency they encounter. Fill them with courage and sustain them with Your peace and comfort. Amen.

DAY 16

BEACON

For we must consider that we shall be a city upon a hill.
The eyes of all people are upon us. . . .

—JOHN WINTHROP, LAWYER AND FIRST GOVERNOR OF MASSACHUSETTS BAY COLONY, 1630

Taking care of the land we've been given is an act of worship. Being grateful for godly leadership is an offering of praise. Honoring God through prayer is the way our nation puts Him first. The seeds of prosperity are sown through hearts of humility, and as we surrender to God's will, we secure a harvest of His goodness for generations to come. Having a reverence for God and a respect for all He's given makes our country shine with a divine light that's impossible to ignore. In attempts to be a beacon to the world, we pray as the psalmist writes, "God be merciful to us and bless us, And cause His face to shine upon us, That Your way may be known on earth, Your salvation among all nations" (Psalm 67:1–2).

Division dims our reflection of God's glory. Wedges between us widen the enemy's hold on our nation. We fall into the darkness we're praying to defeat if we don't determine to stand together and work through our differences. We must allow love to ignite this truth, spoken by the apostle Paul:

> God is at work within you, helping you want to obey him, and then helping you do what he wants. In everything you do, stay away from complaining and arguing so that no one can speak a word of blame against you. You are to live clean, innocent lives as children of God in a dark world full of people who are crooked and stubborn. Shine out among them like beacon lights, holding out to them the Word of Life. (Philippians 2:13–16, TLB)

You are the light of the world. A city that is set on a hill cannot be hidden. Nor do they light a lamp and put it under a basket, but on a lampstand, and it gives light to all who are in the house. Let your light so shine before men, that they may see your good works and glorify your Father in heaven.

—MATTHEW 5:14–16

REFLECT

How will love shine from your life this week?

What areas might God help you with so your life is a clearer reflection of His love?

Have you stumbled in your attempts to be patient and longsuffering with someone who thinks differently than you do? What would a loving, God-honoring response look like?

PRAY

Father, let the light of Your love begin with me as our nation battles the enemies of strife and division. Fill me with Your gentleness, grace, and patience. Let the Holy Spirit guide my thoughts, words, and actions today. Amen.

S. PERCY BARTHOLO

EDWARD MARIA WINGFIELD

WITH TWENTY FIVE OTHERS

WHO

CALLING THE PLACE

"CAPE HENRY"

PLANTED A CROSS

APRIL 29, 1607.

"DEI GRATIA VIRGINIA CONDITA"

THIS TABLET

IS ERECTED BY THE

ASSOCIATION

FOR

VATION OF VIRGINIA ANTI

APRIL 29 1896

DAY 17

COVENANT

We do hereby dedicate this Land, and ourselves, to reach the people within these shores with the Gospel of Jesus Christ, and to raise up Godly generations after us, and with these generations take the Kingdom of God to all the earth. May this Covenant of Dedication remain to all generations, as long as this earth remains, and may this Land, along with England, be Evangelist to the World. May all who see this Cross, remember what we have done here, and may those who come here to inhabit join in this Covenant and in this most noble work that the Holy Scriptures may be fulfilled.

—REVEREND ROBERT HUNT, FIRST LANDING COVENANT AT CAPE HENRY, VIRGINIA, 1607

This is a powerful prayer of dedication that was offered as a covering over our nation, and it's one we should not lose sight of. The men and women who arrived here with the hope of freedom and the fear of God in their hearts prayed for future generations. We should have the same determination. "The counsel of the Lord stands forever, The plans of His heart to all generations. Blessed is the nation whose God is the Lord, The people He has chosen as His own inheritance" (Psalm 33:11–12).

Reverend Robert Hunt asked God to raise up godly generations to take the good news of the gospel to all the earth from the soil he stood upon. Through countless church and missionary organizations we exercise the freedom to do that, and it should never be taken for granted. God blesses this nation through outstretched hands—and God's goodness reaches this country through the covenant promise He made to Abraham: "I will bless those who bless you and curse those who curse you; and the entire world will be blessed because of you" (Genesis 12:3, TLB). Since time began, surrender and obedience have ushered the blessings of heaven to earth through hearts that serve Him. Gratefully, we have inherited the promise.

When Jesus was asked about the most important of all the commandments, *Love God with all your heart, soul, and mind* came in first place. *Love your neighbor as much as you love yourself* was a close second. Love is the most important act of obedience . . . and it opens the door to the greatest blessings of God.

May the God of peace who brought up our Lord Jesus from the dead, that great Shepherd of the sheep, through the blood of the everlasting covenant, make you complete in every good work to do His will, working in you what is well pleasing in His sight, through Jesus Christ, to whom be glory forever and ever.

—HEBREWS 13:20–21

REFLECT

God's love is the reason we have a new covenant. In what ways are you able to spread the love of God from where you are?

Through Jesus Christ, a new covenant was established, offering forgiveness and salvation to all who believe. How might you offer forgiveness to someone in your community?

How will you put God's love into action in your city this week?

PRAY

Father, I praise You for the new covenant we have in Jesus. Fill my heart and mind with the desire to do Your will, obey Your commandments, and be an ambassador of Your love on earth. Bestow grace, humility, and safety upon our U.S. Ambassadors and other Foreign Service members around the globe. Amen.

DAY 18

DEFEND

"This We'll Defend"

—UNITED STATES ARMY MOTTO, 1778

On June 14, 1775, the Continental Army became the first national institution, more than a year before the United States of America declared independence. Congress adopted the New England Army of Observation, which represented all 13 colonies and became a unified fighting force in defense of our freedom. The motto typically emphasizes "WE" rather than "I" to reinforce a fundamental belief in teamwork and selfless service. This motto also signifies a dedication to defending the nation's highest ideals: freedom, democracy, and justice. We pray with the psalmist, "Defend your people, Lord; defend and bless your chosen ones. Lead them like a shepherd and carry them forever in your arms" (Psalm 28:9, TLB).

Charles Spurgeon put it plainly: "As a soldier in battle must never lay aside his shield, so must we never have the word of God out of our minds." "For the word of God is living and powerful, and sharper than any two-edged sword, piercing even to the division of soul and spirit, and of joints and marrow, and is a discerner of thoughts and intents of the heart" (Hebrews 4:12).

We fight a constant battle against the enemy of our souls. If we don't depend on God to overcome, through the knowledge and obedience of His word, we risk losing the hope that has carried our nation this far. The word of God within us is the only way to defeat any threat. "Every word of God is pure; He is a shield to those who put their trust in Him" (Proverbs 30:5). Our greatest defense lies in our daily dependence on the Creator of heaven and earth, whose truth still reigns: "Do not be afraid nor dismayed . . . for the battle is not yours, but God's" (2 Chronicles 20:15).

Deliver me from my enemies, O my God; Defend me from those who rise up against me.

—PSALM 59:1

REFLECT

How does knowing God's Word will not return void inspire you to be a lifelong student of the Bible?

What are important Scriptures for you to pray when you feel weary?

How do you depend on God to defend your peace? How do you depend on the Holy Spirit to comfort and calm you?

REFLECT

Father, I pray for those who participate in military branches that defend our nation. May you give them stamina, strength, peace, guidance, and protection as they serve. Bless and protect their families, meeting all of their needs each day. Amen.

DAY 19

EQUALITY

The genuine equality of human nature is the true principle of all our Rights and duties to one another . . . [I]t really means little more than that we are all of the same species; made by the same God; possessed of minds and bodies alike in essence; having all the same reason, passions, affections, and appetites.

—JOHN ADAMS, FOUNDING FATHER AND SECOND U.S. PRESIDENT, 1794

Equality begins with the truth that all human beings are created by God with the sole duty to love one another. Nothing matters more than our love for God expressing itself through a mutual respect for one another—an inherent characteristic of love. "There is no partiality with God" (Romans 2:11). America's only hope for the hearts and minds of its citizens to see each other through a divine lens will be through the power of prayer. And it will be God's doing. He alone is our hope for love to prevail in this world.

As a nation, we reach a better place and attain a clearer image of our Creator through constant communication with Him. "In everything, by prayer and supplication, with thanksgiving, let your requests be made known to God" (Philippians 4:6). Division is a death blow to *any* nation's hope for genuine equality. The sin of pride is a direct road to division. Our love for God compels us to a life of humility and should, as a result, extinguish any trace of arrogance or sense of superiority. "We are one in Christ Jesus" (Galatians 3:28, TLB).

When we fully understand it's impossible for one of us to be more valuable to God than another, love will lift us above hate, unity will disarm division, and compassion will conquer fear. "Though I have all faith, so that I could remove mountains, but have not love, I am nothing" (1 Corinthians 13:2).

God shows no partiality. But in every nation whoever fears Him and works righteousness is accepted by Him.

—ACTS 10:34-35

REFLECT

What experience has helped you see others the way God sees them?

What are the most significant barriers to reaching genuine equality in the United States today?

In what ways do you think you can be a part of healing the division in our nation?

PRAY

Father, give us, as one people, eyes to see others the way you do, and compassion to love each person we encounter as You would. Impart a heart of humility to our legislators as they work for our good and Your glory. Amen.

DAY 20

CHARITY

With malice toward none with charity for all with firmness in the right as God gives us to see the right let us strive on to finish the work we are in to bind up the nation's wounds, to care for him who shall have borne the battle and for his widow and his orphan—to do all which may achieve and cherish a just and lasting peace among ourselves and with all nations.

—ABRAHAM LINCOLN, SIXTEENTH U.S. PRESIDENT, 1865

The hand of God has carried our nation through times of suffering, uncertainty, and fear. We see the fight against the weapons of darkness rage on, fueled by the abandonment of godliness, the promotion of self-centered thinking, and a lack of love and charity. God has not turned His back on us, even though in great measure, we've turned away from Him.

J. Hudson Taylor, a nineteenth-century missionary, wrote, "If we want to see mighty wonders of divine power and grace wrought in the place of weakness, failure, and disappointment, let us answer God's standing challenge, '*Call unto Me, and I will answer thee, and show thee great and mighty things which thou knowest not!*' " It's no small thing to take up God's challenge for us to cry out to Him in our time of need, and it is not an unreasonable thing to stand together and expect Him to answer.

God has a heart for charity and those who extend it. He makes this clear in Isaiah 58. When a nation treats their people fairly, feeds the hungry, and houses those who are helpless, poor, and destitute, His light will wash over them. Isaiah 58:8–9a (TLB) says, "If you do these things, God will shed his own glorious light upon you. He will heal you; your godliness will lead you forward, goodness will be a shield before you, and the glory of the Lord will protect you from behind. Then, when you call, the Lord will answer, 'Yes, I am here.'" Godliness will always be the best way forward for our nation, and love is its driving force.

I [Paul] was a constant example to you in helping the poor, for I remembered the words of the Lord Jesus, "It is more blessed to give than to receive."

—ACTS 20:35, TLB

REFLECT

When is the last time you participated in charity, an act of compassion without any expectation of receiving something in return?

Ask the Holy Spirit to give you a constant awareness of the needs around you. Listen carefully and record what you hear.

How has God blessed you in response to your acts of giving?

PRAY

Father, may we be a nation filled with charitable hearts and open hands. Let Your compassion guide our giving and inspire our leaders to honor You in their treatment of those they serve. Bless nonprofit organizations that genuinely support, teach, and offer encouragement in this city and throughout this nation. Amen.

DAY 21

MIRACLE

I do not believe that the Constitution was the offspring of inspiration, but I am as perfectly satisfied that the Union of States in its form and adoption is as much the work of a Divine Providence as any of the miracles recorded in the Old and New Testament were the effects of a Divine power.

—DR. BENJAMIN RUSH, FOUNDING FATHER,
SIGNER OF THE DECLARATION OF INDEPENDENCE,
AND ABOLITIONIST, 1788

At a time in our nation when it's difficult to see the unfailing love of God through the divisiveness and darkening news cycles, our prayers for a *miraculous* move of God are paramount. We must join together in this singular outcry. Supporters of the U.S. Constitution saw that the Union of States was divinely ordered. All hope to correct our course rests in God alone.

A. C. Dixon, a pastor in the late nineteenth and early twentieth centuries, wrote, "When we depend on man, we get what man can do; when we depend on prayer, we get what God can do." From the dawn of the country we now celebrate as home, evidence of God's mercy is undeniable. He is in the business of miracles. The sheer wealth of natural beauty we've been given is a reflection of His own. We witness God's grace extended to us daily even in the multitude of our sins, the exclusion of His truth, and the neglect of His commandment to love one another. Every prayer we utter should begin with humility, praise, and *deep gratitude.*

In order to become a nation empowered by love as opposed to one divided by the determination to be right over holy, proud over humble, and intelligent over wise, we are impelled to pray for a miracle. God is the only One who can do it, and our prayers are the only reason He will. In the words of the prophet Jeremiah, "You have all wisdom and do great and mighty miracles; for your eyes are open to all the ways of men, and you reward everyone according to his life and deeds" (Jeremiah 32:19, TLB).

This was the LORD's doing;
It is marvelous in our eyes.

—PSALM 118:23

REFLECT

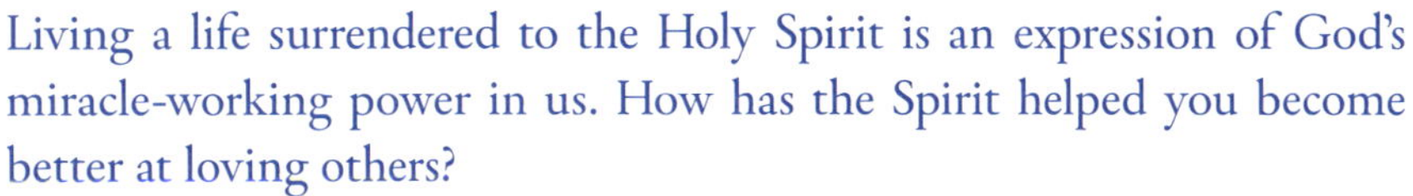

Living a life surrendered to the Holy Spirit is an expression of God's miracle-working power in us. How has the Spirit helped you become better at loving others?

Why might it be difficult for you to remain self-controlled and loving toward those who disagree with you?

Write a short prayer asking God for wisdom and help to unite our communities and the nation in small, practical ways.

PRAY

Father, make our country strong in Your hands. May our goals be shaped by Your will; may our resolve be based in Your truth; may our resources be used for Your glory and the good of others. Cover us with grace, shield us with mercy, and motivate us with love. Amen.

DAY 22

GRACE

O beautiful for spacious skies,
For amber waves of grain,
For purple mountain majesties
Above the fruited plain!
America! America!
God shed His grace on thee
And crown thy good with brotherhood
From sea to shining sea!

—"AMERICA THE BEAUTIFUL," FIRST VERSE,
KATHERINE LEE BATES, 1893

Grace is the unmerited favor of God. Salvation is the greatest proof of that favor upon us, as a people and a nation; it is a gift we did nothing to deserve. Yet without question, accepting God's gift of salvation through the blood of Jesus Christ changes *everything* for humankind. We go from searching for purpose to discovering a call to daily deflection of self-centered pursuits—a mission to serve others for the glory of God. Grace leads to the most fulfilling life possible.

The psalmist writes, "Who can forget the wonders he performs—deeds of mercy and of grace?" (Psalm 111:4, TLB). Revisiting times in U.S. history when God's grace shined brightly through our leaders is an important way to remain mindful of this gift. Upon designating a Day of National Humiliation, Fasting, and Prayer in 1863, President Lincoln proclaimed:

> We have been the recipients of the choicest bounties of Heaven. We have been preserved these many years in peace and prosperity. We have grown in numbers, wealth, and power as no other nation has ever grown. But we have forgotten God. We have forgotten the gracious Hand which preserved us in peace, and multiplied and enriched and strengthened us; and we have vainly imagined, in the deceitfulness of our hearts, that all these blessings were produced by some superior wisdom and virtue of our own.

In 1988, President Reagan permanently set the National Day of Prayer as the first Thursday of every May. Joining in prayer as one people is the single most powerful weapon we have against the enemy of God's goodness and grace.

Having been justified by faith, we have peace with God through our Lord Jesus Christ, through whom also we have access by faith into this grace in which we stand, and rejoice in hope of the glory of God.

—ROMANS 5:1–2

REFLECT

What does the free gift of grace mean to you?

When you see God's favor in your life, what is your response?

How have you witnessed the grace and mercy God has poured out on our nation?

PRAY

Father, thank You for this nation and the people you've put in place to lead it. Thank you for pouring out grace upon our land. Let your favor flow from heaven as we lift our eyes to You for new mercies every morning. Amen.

DAY 23

RIGHTS

We hold these truths to be self-evident, that all men are created equal, that they are endowed by their Creator with certain unalienable Rights, that among these are Life, Liberty, and the Pursuit of Happiness.

—THE UNITED STATES OF AMERICA'S DECLARATION OF INDEPENDENCE, 1776

With the breath of God in every human's lungs come the unalienable rights pronounced in our Declaration of Independence: Life, Liberty, and the Pursuit of Happiness. We have the freedom to pursue a life of obedience to God and the blessing that follows. It's the only life that leads to true happiness and contentment. A life that honors God is filled with dreams that glorify God. Our innate purpose is designed to uplift the greatest commandments, which all others depend on: to love God and to love our neighbor.

We are made in the image of our Creator—miraculously, lovingly, and purposefully. That truth alone renders every life priceless. Our worth as individuals, and collectively as a nation *held together* by love and truth, is found in the heart of God. Our God says, "Before I formed you in the womb I knew you; Before you were born I sanctified you" (Jeremiah 1:5). We are set apart for all God created us to be. Every fiber of our being has been knit together by His love. No one else loves us more, defines our value, or fulfills our deepest longings. We belong to God, and from the moment we take our first breath our spirit pines for a relationship with Him. Jesus gave His life to usher us into the place of true belonging—the arms of our heavenly Father.

Our hope to pull this country together and enjoy the rights that come with the gift of freedom—the very thing our founders knew was our sustaining strength—can be found in God alone.

He will listen to the prayers of the destitute, for he is never too busy to heed their requests. I am recording this so that future generations will also praise the Lord for all that he has done. And the people that shall be created shall praise the Lord.

—PSALM 102:17–18, TLB

REFLECT

The idea of rights is rooted in Christian theology and morality. The foundational principle, *Imago Dei* (or image of God), is based on Genesis 1:26. When you reflect on your infinite worth to your heavenly Father, how does it affect the way you see others?

What moves you to compassion for your fellow man?

Who has God brought into your life as inspiration to be more loving and compassionate?

PRAY

Father, extinguish the embers of division and hatred in our nation. Use me to be Your messenger of love, unity, and respect for the rights and lives of others. Amen.

People
provide for the
establish this

DAY 24

CONSTITUTION

We the People of the United States, in Order to form a more perfect Union, establish Justice, insure domestic Tranquility, provide for the common defense, promote the general Welfare, and secure the Blessings of Liberty to ourselves and our Posterity, do ordain and establish this Constitution for the United States of America.

—THE CONSTITUTION OF THE UNITED STATES OF AMERICA, 1787

★ ★ ★ ★ ★

Since the signing of our Constitution on September 17, 1787, we as a people have been praying for the divine intervention that will make us a "more perfect union." God is the only One who makes it possible to reach our aspirations. "He is the Rock, His work is perfect; For all His ways are justice, A God of truth and without injustice; Righteous and upright is He" (Deuteronomy 32:4).

Our human imperfection is an ongoing threat to the justice, tranquility, and general welfare that the authors of our Constitution hoped for. But because our prayers rise to the throne room, fall on our Savior's ears, and open the Father's heart, hope endures. If our country is to secure the blessings of liberty to ourselves and our posterity, it is imperative that we call on God without ceasing. Prayer reflects humility, an understanding that by our own will we are powerless to live the life Jesus died to give us—one of supernatural peace and eternal hope.

Tribulations are part of life, and they will continue to be part of our growth as a country. God's timing and the depth of suffering we experience are often beyond our understanding. God's hand of judgement is restrained by a compassion for the lost that we *cannot* fathom, and the boundless grace we're all indebted to through the sacrifice of Jesus Christ. In these times, we *must* trust God with a renewed determination and be encouraged by the words of Pastor J. Sidlow Baxter, who said, "Men may spurn our appeals, reject our message, oppose our arguments, and despise our persons, but they are helpless against our prayers."

I exhort first of all that supplications, prayers, intercessions, and giving of thanks be made for all men . . . and all who are in authority, that we may lead a quiet and peaceable life in all godliness and reverence.

—1 TIMOTHY 2:1–2

REFLECT

How can you become more familiar with the U.S. Constitution as you intercede for our nation?

How might you promote peace, understanding, and love within the circle of those you know?

How is your prayer life influenced by the hope you have for future generations and God's continued faithfulness to our country?

PRAY

Father, we know that as a land, a nation, and a people, there is nothing greater than Your presence with us and Your favor upon us. May we move ahead with faith and reliance upon You in all things and at all times. May we live in such a way that pleases You and blesses America. Amen.

DAY 25

HEALING

Let us, then, fellow citizens, unite with one heart and one mind. Let us restore to social intercourse that harmony and affection without which liberty and even life itself are but dreary things.

—THOMAS JEFFERSON, THIRD U.S. PRESIDENT, 1801

Our sins as a nation cloud our vision of unity. True repentance draws us closer to God. In losing sight of the unifying power of love, humanity suffers from the blindness we create, and healing can seem an impossible process. The attributes of love are, at their core, the balm that can heal the deepest wounds caused by turning away from God. As the apostle Paul wrote, "Love suffers long and is kind; love does not envy; love does not parade itself, is not puffed up; does not behave rudely, does not seek its own, is not provoked, thinks no evil; does not rejoice in iniquity, but rejoices in the truth" (1 Corinthians 13:4–6).

Abraham Lincoln, when calling for the nation to pray for forgiveness, wrote, "In sincerity and truth, let us then rest humbly in the hope authorized by the Divine teachings, that the united cry of the nation will be heard on high and answered with blessing no less than the pardon of our national sins and the restoration of our now divided and suffering country to its former happy condition of unity and peace." Because healing as a nation begins with individual healing, the work of restoration starts with a quiet look within. We become whole by humbling ourselves before the Lord, and we are united by becoming a clearer reflection of Christ every day. Let us pray as King David once prayed, "Lord, restore us again to your favor" (Psalm 60:1, TLB).

I am the LORD who heals you.

—EXODUS 15:26b

REFLECT

What needs healing within your own heart?

Has the Holy Spirit shown you one relationship in your life that needs prayer and healing?

In what ways has God healed you by revealing His love and forgiveness?

PRAY

Father, heal me. Heal my family. Heal my neighborhood. Provide citizens in this nation a self-awareness, through the Holy Spirit, to see our weaknesses and learn how to love You more and love others with kindness and compassion. Bring healing to our land. Amen.

DAY 26

BLESSING

I pray heaven to bestow the best of blessings on this house and all that shall hereafter inhabit it. May none but honest and wise men ever rule under this roof.

—PRESIDENT JOHN ADAMS'S BLESSING ENGRAVED ON THE MANTEL IN THE STATE DINING ROOM OF THE WHITE HOUSE, 1800

The blessing of God comes to a nation through those who prayerfully lead it and the people who humbly fear the Lord. Prioritizing God is at the heart of a strong nation. In these trying times, we're seeing the spiritual battle intensify for the soul of America. We're in the fight of our lives for the life of our nation. What can we do from where we are? We can remain steadfast in prayer. We can be humble, loving, and kind. We can be quick to forgive and willing to admit when we're wrong. We can see a need and meet that need in the name of Jesus. James, the brother of Jesus, encourages readers to "Confess your trespasses to one another, and pray for one another, that you may be healed. The effective, fervent prayer of a righteous man avails much" (James 5:16).

John Adams prayed a blessing over the White House in 1800. He called on God to raise up leaders who exemplify the virtues of wisdom and honesty. As fellow Americans, we can stand in agreement with President Adams's prayer today. Our hope is not in human efforts or accomplishments. Our hope is in the God of heaven and earth, who can be trusted to carry us forward with the same faithfulness that has brought us this far. "Blessed is the man who fears the LORD, Who delights greatly in His commandments. His descendants will be mighty on earth; The generation of the upright will be blessed" (Psalm 112:1–2). When we stand on God's promise to bless us, we commit to a life in His service, surrendered to His absolute authority and perfect will.

Blessed is the nation whose God is the LORD,
The people He has chosen as His own inheritance.

—PSALM 33:12

REFLECT

From your perspective, what are the greatest blessings God has given our country?

What do you appreciate most about calling the United States your home?

What guidance or blessings do you ask God to pour out on our nation during these trying times?

PRAY

Father, we know Your goodness is the light that shines through the darkness, and nothing will overcome Your light. Bless our nation as we obey the commandment to serve You by loving one another. Amen.

DAY 27

RISK

We live in continual expectation of hostilities. Scarcely a day that does not produce some; but, like good Nehemiah, having made our prayer unto God, and set the people with their swords, their spears, and their bows, we will say unto them, "Be ye not afraid of them; remember the Lord, who is great and terrible, and fight for your brethren, your sons, and your daughters, your wives and your houses."

—ABIGAIL ADAMS, SECOND FIRST LADY OF THE UNITED STATES, 1775

We have an enemy who does not sleep, but we serve the God Almighty who is awake, aware, and all-powerful. "These things I have spoken to you, that in Me you may have peace. In the world you will have tribulation; but be of good cheer, I have overcome the world" (John 16:33). Risk is part of being a child of God. Risk is being exposed to loss. When we give our lives to Christ, we lose our own. It's a state of constant surrender. The Holy Spirit infuses us with the courage to do it, because we're helpless to draw that kind of strength on our own.

We're alive at this time in history *for a purpose*. As our ancestors did, we can go fearlessly into the days God planned for us, trusting Him wholeheartedly. Economic, political, environmental, security, and social risks face our nation, but we are not without hope. Jesus asked, "Are not two sparrows sold for a copper coin?" He followed that by saying, "Not one of them falls to the ground apart from your Father's will." To expound on the truth that God pays close attention to our lives and is in complete control, Jesus added, "The very hairs of your head are all numbered. Do not fear therefore; you are of more value than many sparrows" (Matthew 10:29–31).

We risk far more by living a life that *isn't* fully committed to God, entrusted in His hands, and laid at His feet. "He who does not take his cross and follow after Me is not worthy of Me. He who finds his life will lose it, and he who loses his life for My sake will find it" (Matthew 10:38–39).

I will praise the Lord no matter what happens. I will constantly speak of His glories and grace.

—PSALM 34:1, TLB

REFLECT

What areas of your life are hardest to surrender to God?

In our humanness, letting go of control feels like a risk. What have you turned over to God because it was impossible to control?

How do you face situations where you risk losing something? In what ways has this built your trust in God?

PRAY

Father, increase our courage as a nation to put our trust in Your perfect love and sovereignty. Shift our eyes from any risk or terror, to Jesus. Give us grace and confidence to accept the risks we take in speaking His name, defending truth, and surrendering everything to You. Amen.

DAY 28

LOYALTY

The Declaration of Independence is the ring-bolt to the chain of your nation's destiny; so indeed, I regard it. The principles contained in that instrument are saving principles, be true to them on all occasions, in all places, against all foes, and at whatever cost.

—FREDERICK DOUGLASS, FORMER SLAVE, MINISTER, AND ABOLITIONIST, 1852

The U.S. Declaration of Independence begins with truths for *every* citizen, as we are *equally* valuable gifts from our Creator. We have rights, endowed by the One who stitched us together in our mother's womb, that cannot be stripped away. God is the Author of every life. He is the only way to true liberty, and He is the reward of every pursuit that leads to a blessed life.

Frederick Douglass was born at a time when the sins of our nation threatened the very principles set forth in the declaration signed by representatives from the original thirteen colonies. He suffered unspeakable atrocities during that dark time, yet he knew the truths in our Declaration of Independence, penned over forty years before his birth, had the power to save our divided country if they were upheld. By the grace of God they were, and a crippled nation moved forward. We continue the work of ushering in healing.

The Declaration of Independence concludes with: "And for support of this declaration, with a firm reliance on the protection of divine Providence, we mutually pledge to each other our Lives, our Fortunes, and our sacred Honor." Loyalty means to demonstrate faithful devotion, commitment, and unwavering support to a person, group, or idea—even during difficult times. It was God who gave our forefathers the courage to enter the deep, abiding commitment to declare our freedom, and it is God alone who will continue to heal our nation as we maintain loyalty to Him and one another. A firm reliance on Him is our only reliable hope to stand by one another and uphold connection over division.

Oh, love the Lord, all of you who are his people; for the Lord protects those who are loyal to him.

—PSALM 31:23a, TLB

REFLECT

Why do you think loyalty to the Holy Trinity is important?

How does loyalty to the Father, Son, and Holy Spirit impact being an American citizen?

How can you align your thoughts and actions with God's love for the unity of our country?

PRAY

Father, let me be loyal first and foremost to You and Your holy word. Help me participate in healing our nation by loving my fellow citizens. Give me courage and a renewed commitment to the power of Your love to unite us. Amen.

DAY 29

MIGHTY OAK

The oak tree will now be as much a symbol of America as Thanksgiving Day, Old Glory, The Star Spangled Banner, and the bald eagle. It is a fine choice to represent our nation's strength, as it grows from just an acorn into a powerful entity whose many branches continue to strengthen and reach skyward with every passing year.

—BEN NELSON, FORMER GOVERNOR OF NEBRASKA AND U.S. SENATOR, 2004

The oak became America's National Tree in 2004. Often called the "mighty oak" because of its deep roots, spectacular size, and longevity, the oak tree is a symbol of strength, endurance, and resilience.

Historically, oak trees provided materials for making ink. The ink derived from oak galls produced a more permanent jet-black color—and it's the iron gall ink that was used to pen the earliest complete Bible. The word of God is the pillar of our strength, endurance, and resilience. God used the natural world He created as a means to record His living and active Word—first transcribed on scrolls, now engraved on our hearts. It is the foundation of our existence as a people and a country. The apostle Paul wrote: "[Others] can see that you are a letter from Christ. . . . It is not a letter written with pen and ink, but by the Spirit of the living God; not one carved on stone, but in human hearts" (2 Corinthians 3:3, TLB).

The mighty oak is long-lived, supports a greater diversity of life than any other tree, and is called a "keystone" species because it's an exceptionally large part of supporting the entire ecosystem. God created the oak as He did our country—to be a vital part of an earthly system. We are diverse, strong, and supportive. We are a powerful nation, central to the well-being of our friends and allies around the world.

God rooted America in His mercy and love to be a place of refuge, a tower of strength, and a land from which His light shines and His word goes forth. "Let your roots grow down into him and draw up nourishment from him. See that you go on growing in the Lord, and become strong and vigorous in the truth you were taught" (Colossians 2:7a, TLB).

He will give: beauty for ashes; joy instead of mourning; praise instead of heaviness. For God has planted them like strong and graceful oaks for his own glory.

—ISAIAH 61:3, TLB

REFLECT

How healthy are your spiritual roots right now?

In what ways do you think you need to grow in the Lord and become stronger?

When have you felt your spiritual roots deepen?

PRAY

Father, I'm grateful for the gift of faith. Help my belief deepen, and secure this nation in You, Your word, and Your favor. I ask for an outpouring of Your Spirit in hearts, homes, and neighborhoods—north to south, east to west. May Your name be praised throughout our land and around the globe. Amen.

DAY 30

MERCY

O beautiful for heroes proved in liberating strife,
Who more than self their country loved, and mercy more than life!
America, America! May God thy gold refine,
Till all success, be nobleness, and every gain divine.

—"AMERICA THE BEAUTIFUL," THIRD VERSE,
KATHERINE LEE BATES, 1893

We enjoy the freedom to worship God and to pursue the desires He puts in our hearts because there have been heroes who believed those liberties were worth their lives. "Precious in the sight of the LORD is the death of His saints" (Psalm 116:15). When a life lived for God is over, our hearts should compel us to look for God's mercy. It is here. The plans and purposes of God matter most—and they are *saturated* in His mercy.

For the *greatest* good of the *highest* number of people, God orchestrates His plans on earth. That's what perfect love does. Look for the beauty of God's mercy in *everything*. In our tribulations, we may not be given the discernment to trace His hand, but He will never be slack in sustaining us. "Through the LORD's mercies we are not consumed, Because His compassions fail not" (Lamentations 3:22).

The birth and life of the United States are God's doing, and He can be trusted with our future. It's up to us to surrender it to Him in prayer. We can't know what lies ahead, but we can know the One who does. Jesus said, "And this is eternal life, that they may know You, the only true God, and Jesus Christ whom You have sent" (John 17:3). Our love for God, our compassion for one another, and our basic human need for community—an innate desire given to us by our Creator—are what will bind us together. "Let Your mercy, O LORD, be upon us, Just as we hope in You" (Psalm 33:22)

Let not mercy and truth forsake you;
Bind them around your neck,
Write them on the tablet of your heart.

—PROVERBS 3:3

REFLECT

The Lord's mercies are new every morning. How have you recently been challenged to show mercy?

When has mercy been extended to you?

How might America do a better job of showing mercy to its citizens? To the citizens of the world?

PRAY

Father, as a country You've birthed and blessed us. Grant us a mercy like Your own—without limits. To the undeserving, to those who don't know You, may we be the light that leads to You. I lift up my church, the churches of this city, and nonprofit organizations of our nation who show mercy each day. Bless each one with resources, endurance, and encouragement as expressions of Your loving character. Amen.

DAY 31

LIFE

With consistency, beautiful and undeviating, human life, from its commencement to its close, is protected by the Common Law.

—JAMES WILSON, SIGNER OF THE DECLARATION OF INDEPENDENCE AND THE U.S. CONSTITUTION, AND AN ORIGINAL JUSTICE OF THE U.S. SUPREME COURT, 1790–91

Life is a gift from God. James Wilson supported life "from its commencement," beginning in the womb as described in Psalm 139, "to its close" being supported by Common Law. Without question and without exception, *every life is priceless*. Our worth is not measured by our good deeds, right decisions, or any sense of moral superiority we might conclude we've reached by human efforts. Our worth is measured by our Creator. It is infinite and beyond our comprehension. As the people of an independent nation, we cannot forget we are dependent on a sovereign God. We are here because we are His creation. Any denial of that truth is a departure from those who saw this nation overcome obstacles and attempts to prevent its existence as a free country.

The apostle Paul reminds us,

> Because of his kindness, you have been saved through trusting Christ. And even trusting is not of yourselves; it too is a gift from God. Salvation is not a reward for the good we have done, so none of us can take any credit for it. It is God himself who has made us what we are and given us new lives from Christ Jesus; and long ages ago he planned that we should spend these lives in helping others. (Ephesians 2:8–10, TLB)

Try to imagine what kind of country we would have if every citizen spent their life serving God and helping others.

If we are desperate enough to move toward that degree of love in action, we begin by surrendering every aspect of life to God's will each day. Love can become an unstoppable sweeping movement across our nation—and the world—if each one of us takes this call literally and intentionally. Together, love prevails and God is praised.

He gives to all life, breath, and all things. And He has made from one blood every nation of men to dwell on all the face of the earth, and has determined their preappointed times and the boundaries of their dwellings, so that they should seek the Lord, in the hope that they might grope for Him and find Him, though He is not far from each one of us; for in Him we live and move and have our being.

—ACTS 17:25b–28a

REFLECT

The "American Dream" is opportunity for personal advancement and a free life. How has this been a positive ideal for our country? How has this ideal negatively impacted society?

Define a rich life as an American citizen.

What has God done in your life and in your spirit that makes you most thankful?

PRAY

Father, thank You for creating life and giving my life purpose. Help me to use my life for the good of all and the glory that is Yours. Let our country's collective cry begin with me. Hear us and hold us as we serve You with every breath. May we esteem life and its value each day. Amen.

PROCEEDINGS
OF THE
Virginia Assembly

DAY 32

BOLD

Gentlemen may cry, Peace, Peace—but there is no peace.
The war is actually begun! . . .
Is life so dear, or peace so sweet,
as to be purchased at the price of chains and slavery?
Forbid it, Almighty God!
I know not what course others may take;
but as for me, give me liberty or give me death!

—PATRICK HENRY, LAWYER AND MEMBER OF THE CONTINENTAL CONGRESS, 1775

Patrick Henry was passionate about the path he envisioned for America, and he cried out to Almighty God with a willingness to give his life to pave the way. Countless others would follow with the willingness to sacrifice everything for future generations. It was with faith and bravery that the United States gained its independence.

Today, the hope of our founders' vision stays alive through our willingness to stand on truth. "Now, Lord . . . grant to Your servants that with all boldness they may speak Your word" (Acts 4:29). This nation was founded for the good of its people and the glory of God. He alone will be our light in the darkness. "Your word is a lamp to my feet And a light to my path" (Psalm 119:105).

The courage to establish the course of our nation came from the God who never changes. He provided wisdom, vision, and bold convictions to those whose aim was to live out Jesus's instruction to Christians to be a "city on a hill" (see Matthew 5:14–16) and live in the liberty only Christ can offer. God is faithful, and trusting Him is invaluable. We, like the psalmist, can say, "In the day I cried out, You answered me, And made me bold with strength in my soul" (Psalm 138:3).

Our prayers are as much a lifeline now as they were when the Founding Fathers cried out for God. We are more distracted than we've ever been by technology and the cares of this world. But the word of God is still our life support. Our liberties align with truth and our determination to uphold it. "I will walk at liberty, for I seek Your precepts" (Psalm 119:45).

The wicked flee when no one pursues, but the righteous are bold as a lion.

—PROVERBS 28:1

REFLECT

What biblical figures encourage you to be bold for God's glory?

How do you see the wisdom of God increasing in your life?

What three things will you plead for on behalf of this country in your prayer time today?

PRAY

Father, I want to be disciplined in filling my heart and mind with truth. Help my unbelief! Guide me in living boldly for You. Following You is my first priority. Let me be part of our nation's renewed commitment to exalt You and give You the glory due Your name. Amen.

DAY 33

ALLEGIANCE

I pledge allegiance to the Flag of the United States of America, and to the Republic for which it stands, one Nation [under God], indivisible, with liberty and justice for all.

—THE PLEDGE OF ALLEGIANCE, FRANCIS BELLAMY, 1892

The founders of our nation held an allegiance to the Creator that preceded their devotion to this country. In no other way could colonies have united and made it through the danger and uncertainty of forging a new nation under God. "O LORD God of our fathers, are You not God in heaven, and do You not rule over all the kingdoms of the nations, and in Your hand is there not power and might, so that no one is able to withstand You?" (2 Chronicles 20:6). Thank God for this republic. This admission is where every prayer for our national interest should start. Gratitude tills the soil of our hearts, making each of us ready to receive what the Holy Spirit wants to increase and grow.

The Pledge of Allegiance was written for a youth publication in 1892. The additional words "under God" were approved during President Eisenhower's term in 1954. Throughout our nation's history, our leaders have honored the truth that this country has been established with a divine and deliberate purpose. Our free and flourishing nation owes its allegiance to the God of heaven and earth. By dwelling in the hearts of those who sailed to our shores in the seventeenth century, God moved to bless the world through the blessings He's given to us.

"You have stored up great blessings for those who trust and reverence You" (Psalm 31:19, TLB). Allegiance to God and country is a commitment we've undertaken as a people for the sake of the continued gifts entrusted to us by our Creator. It is incumbent upon us, who are beneficiaries of God's eternal goodness, to be a nation that prays without ceasing.

Let the world look to Me for salvation! For I am God; there is no other. I have sworn by myself, and I will never go back on My word, for it is true—that every knee in all the world shall bow to Me, and every tongue shall swear allegiance to My name.

—ISAIAH 45:22–24, TLB

REFLECT

Our priorities surface in our words and actions. How does allegiance to God take precedence in your life: thought, word, and deed?

In what areas of life do you feel as the disciples did that you "must obey God rather than men" (Acts 5:29)?

Respecting rulers, obeying laws, and paying taxes are considered part of giving "to Caesar the things that are Caesar's" (Matthew 22:21). How can these duties and our attitudes display the ultimate allegiance to God's kingdom?

PRAY

Father, I ask You to fill the leaders of every state in our union with Your love and wisdom. May the Holy Spirit fall afresh on every elected official. May they hold the conviction that we are under Your authority and none other than You is worthy of our loyalty and praise. Amen.

DAY 34

FAVOR

Annuit coeptis, meaning "God has favored our undertakings."

—INSCRIPTION ON THE U.S. CAPITOL BUILDING ABOVE THE SENATE EAST ENTRANCE

It is our responsibility to choose our leaders through prayerful consideration. Our heart's desire should be for leaders who are God-fearing and committed to doing what's right and true. None will be perfect, but God blesses the righteous—and our righteousness is in Christ Jesus alone.

"For You, O Lord, will bless the righteous; With favor You will surround him as with a shield" (Psalm 5:12). In a perfect world, all those in authority would rejoice in the saving grace of Jesus. In reality, perfection will only be attained when the government rests on the shoulder of perfect love, whose titles will be: " 'Wonderful,' 'Counselor,' 'The Mighty God,' 'The Everlasting Father,' 'The Prince of Peace' " (Isaiah 9:6, TLB).

When our congressional leaders walk into the U.S. Capitol, the words engraved on the building serve as a reminder, and in a sense, they are a silent prayer for all to see. While the inscription may go unnoticed by those who walk beneath it daily, God is active, watching our undertakings as a nation, and His favor follows the faithful. We can pray just as King David did, "I entreated Your favor with my whole heart; Be merciful to me according to Your word" (Psalm 119:58).

When lifting our leaders in prayer, claim the blessing of the Lord as recorded in Numbers 6:24–26 (TLB) and speak God's word over them: "May the Lord bless you and keep you; may the Lord's face radiate with joy because of you; may he be gracious to you, show you his favor, and give you his peace."

Never tire of loyalty and kindness. Hold these virtues tightly. Write them deep within your heart. If you want favor with both God and man, and a reputation for good judgment and common sense, then trust the Lord completely; don't ever trust yourself.

—PROVERBS 3:3–5, TLB

REFLECT

What other Scriptures have you chosen when praying for our leaders?

What does it mean to have God's favor on our nation?

How might you commit to praying for specific individuals who hold elected offices in your city, county, state, and nation?

PRAY

Father, be merciful to our congressional leaders; transform hearts of stone to hearts of flesh so they are tender to Your word. Provide wisdom, clarity, and protection for each individual and their families. Open each person's eyes to understanding and bless our nation with Your favor and goodness through humility and obedience. Amen.

DAY 35

EAGLE

The Founding Fathers made an appropriate choice when they selected the bald eagle as the emblem of the nation. The fierce beauty and proud independence of this great bird aptly symbolizes the strength and freedom of America.

—JOHN F. KENNEDY, THIRTY-FIFTH U.S. PRESIDENT, 1961

The American Bald Eagle has been a national symbol since its appearance on the Great Seal of the United States in 1782. This emblem of our nation reflects strength, power, and independence. The North American continent is the only region bald eagles call home. Like the country it represents, the American Bald Eagle is respected and beautiful, owing its majestic presence to the Creator of all things. Throughout this nation's tumultuous history, leaders and citizens have had ample opportunity to turn back from the fight to survive, grow, and become better. The country has not fled from battles or succumbed to raging storms that threatened the ideals of an independent nation. Like an eagle, the United States protects and shields the vulnerable during storms and attacks by predators, and consistently allows the wind of God's Spirit to raise up its people over impending dangers.

By trusting God, America rose to greater heights, grew through adversity, and continues to strive toward being a place of hope and opportunity for every citizen. While our lives are subject to a short time of earthly citizenship, a heart surrendered to God has much to gain. May we raise this prayer, "Teach us to number our days, That we may gain a heart of wisdom" (Psalm 90:12).

Psalm 103:1–5 offers a perfectly worded expression that we, as one nation, might recite on behalf of this generation and those to come:

> Bless the LORD, O my soul;
> And all that is within me, bless His holy name!
> Bless the LORD, O my soul,
> And forget not all His benefits:
> Who forgives all your iniquities,
> Who heals all your diseases,
> Who redeems your life from destruction,
> Who crowns you with lovingkindness and tender mercies,
> Who satisfies your mouth with good things,
> So that your youth is renewed like the eagle's.

Those who wait on the LORD shall renew their strength; They shall mount up with wings like eagles, They shall run and not be weary, They shall walk and not faint.

—ISAIAH 40:31

REFLECT

What do you believe is our nation's greatest strength?

How does the symbol of an eagle inspire you as a child of God and as an American citizen?

What fears do you have concerning our nation? Offer them to God here and now.

PRAY

Father, I praise You for all You've done to lead our nation through the challenges that rise against us. It is by Your presence, grace, and power that we overcome every obstacle. Help us to keep our eyes upward and trust in Your promise to raise us up on eagles' wings. Amen.

DAY 36

REPUBLIC

In these my confidence will under every difficulty be best placed, next to that which we have all been encouraged to feel in the guardianship and guidance of that Almighty Being whose power regulates the destiny of nations, whose blessings have been so conspicuously dispensed to this rising Republic, and to whom we are bound to address our devout gratitude for the past, as well as our fervent supplications and best hopes for the future.

—JAMES MADISON, FOUNDING FATHER AND FOURTH U.S. PRESIDENT, 1809

James Madison vowed to place his confidence in God under every difficulty. He gave honor to "that Almighty Being whose power regulates the destiny of nations." With these words, President Madison issued a blessing on the rising Republic which had seen the *conspicuous* goodness of our Lord. "Blessed is the man who trusts in the Lord and has made the Lord his hope and confidence" (Jeremiah 17:7, TLB). Trust in God inspires our elected leaders to become greater because love, compassion, and wisdom guide their hearts, minds, and decisions.

On October 6, 1935, President Franklin D. Roosevelt wrote this: "In the formative days of the Republic, the directing influence the Bible exercised upon the fathers of the Nation is conspicuously evident. . . . We cannot read the history of our rise and development as a Nation without reckoning with the place the Bible has occupied in shaping the advances of the Republic." God is not distant and removed from the working of governments, the people in them, or the events that affect our world. Especially in the midst of tribulation and suffering, His purposes are beyond understanding. In our human capacity for reasoning, we want to see His love and justice prevail in every way. "Stand up, O God, and judge the earth. For all of it belongs to you. All nations are in your hands" (Psalm 82:8, TLB).

But our Savior warned there would be dark and troubling times ahead. And He promised, "I am with you always, even to the end of the age" (Matthew 28:20). While building the early church, Paul and Barnabas held to the same truth. They helped the believers to grow in love for God and each other. "They encouraged them to continue in the faith in spite of all the persecution, reminding them that they must enter into the Kingdom of God through many tribulations" (Acts 14:22, TLB). Our Republic is worth preserving—and truth holds the power to sustain it.

Be still, and know that I am God; I will be exalted among the nations, I will be exalted in the earth!

—PSALM 46:10

REFLECT

Our nation can be changed by the power of God's love. What is one small way you can get involved in bringing His love to your neighborhood or community?

When you see the suffering around the globe, how does it guide your prayers?

Find three Bible passages and record them here. Pray these verses over our nation for one week.

PRAY

Father, let Your truth be engraved on the tablet of our hearts. Fill the minds of our leaders with the power of Your word, the wisdom of Your ways, and the love that will change our world. Be present in every area of the legislative, executive, and judicial branches. Administer your final authority throughout the U.S. government and bring unity at the foot of the cross. Amen.

DAY 37

VALOR

Aye! We've been always ready!
To do, to fight, or die
Write glory to the shield we wear
In letters to the sky.
To sink the foe or save the maimed,
Our mission and our pride.
We'll carry on 'til Kingdom Come,
Ideals for which we've died.

—*SEMPER PARATUS (ALWAYS READY)*, FINAL VERSE OF THE U.S. COAST GUARD MARCHING SONG, CAPTAIN FRANCIS SALTUS VAN BOSKERCK, 1922

Thank God for the valor of the men and women who serve our country, daily confronting challenges to save or protect others. Praise Jesus for the courage of their commitment to risk their lives. Give us, Holy Spirit, a constant conviction to cover them in prayer. Each life holds infinite worth, and by the power of God, one life can make all the difference. In Judges 6, an angel of the Lord visited a man named Gideon. He was from the weakest clan, and he was the least in his father's house. The Angel of the Lord appeared to [Gideon] and proclaimed, "The LORD is with you, you mighty man of valor!" (Judges 6:12).

Great courage in the face of danger isn't manmade, it's God-ordained. Our greatest service to our nation is in the spiritual courage we have to stand up for truth. "For you were once darkness, but now you are light in the Lord. Walk as children of light (for the fruit of the Spirit is in all goodness, righteousness, and truth), finding out what is acceptable to the Lord" (Ephesians 5:8–9). "America was born to exemplify that devotion to the elements of righteousness which are derived from the revelations of Holy Scripture," stated President Woodrow Wilson in his address "The Bible and Progress" on May 7, 1911. The moral courage to follow God fearlessly, to pray for His wisdom tirelessly, and to share His love relentlessly, is our divine assignment.

God's plan for each of us to be here at this time in U.S. history holds a greater purpose than we fully know—but we can be fully submitted to it and live out our purpose one day at a time.

In every battle you will need faith as your shield to stop the fiery arrows aimed at you by Satan. And you will need the helmet of salvation and the sword of the Spirit—which is the Word of God. Pray all the time. Ask God for anything in line with the Holy Spirit's wishes. Plead with him, reminding him of your needs, and keep praying earnestly for all Christians everywhere.

—EPHESIANS 6:16–18, TLB

REFLECT

How do you ask God for courage to do His will?

What do you believe is the most important part of God's plan for you?

How can Americans better esteem valor and express gratitude for those protecting the ideals this nation was founded upon?

PRAY

Father, let truth guide us into every purpose You have for this nation. Give those who serve our country fearless hearts and faithful souls. Watch over each individual serving in the Army, Navy, Marine Corps, Air Force, Space Force, and Coast Guard. Protect the family members who support these men and women serving our nation. Richly bless and provide for all the veterans who have given their time and service to this Republic. May You be glorified and honored. Amen.

DAY 38

FLAG

If one asks me the meaning of our flag, I say to him: It means all that the Constitution of our people, organizing for justice, for liberty, and for happiness, meant. Our flag carries American ideas, American history and American feelings. This American flag was the safeguard of liberty. It was an ordinance of liberty by the people, for the people. That it meant, that it means, and, by the blessing of God, that it shall mean to the end of time!

—HENRY WARD BEECHER, MINISTER AND ABOLITIONIST, 1861

Symbols are powerful. They are visual representations of things we believe and hold in high regard. Our flag, sometimes referred to as "Old Glory," is a deeply significant reminder of how our country began and how God has blessed it since. The thirteen stripes stand for the original thirteen colonies. By the bloodshed of the colonists who believed in the God-given rights of every person, the United States of America won its independence. The fifty white stars represent the states of our great nation, which has flourished and grown by God's goodness and guidance.

Henry Ward Beecher eloquently explained the meaning of our flag. He also understood how it has endured and where the praise for it goes when he exclaimed, ". . . by the blessing of God . . . to the end of time!" Our flag should be given honor and respect for the history it represents, the lives sacrificed to uphold its meaning, and the God who births nations on earth for His glory. "I will praise You, O Lord, among the peoples, And I will sing praises to You among the nations" (Psalm 108:3).

When we see the U.S. flag, it should not induce a feeling of indifference. It should inspire us to think about the magnitude of the price paid for our freedom, and the magnificent God who gave individuals the strength to afford it. Our flag flies still, against the blue skies of our beautiful country, for the glory of our faithful God. Our prayers should be for every person it represents—those who sacrificed their lives, those living free lives, and those hoping to taste the freedom of a new life in our blessed and bountiful United States of America.

All the ends of the world shall remember and turn to the LORD, and all the families of the nations shall worship before You. For the kingdom is the LORD's, and He rules over the nations.

—PSALM 22:27–28

REFLECT

The colors of the flag have intentional meaning. Red symbolizes bravery and hardiness; white symbolizes purity and innocence; blue represents vigilance, perseverance, and justice. What emotions do you associate with the American flag?

What does the American flag symbolize to you and why?

How might you pray and lift a banner of God's authority over your life and the United States?

PRAY

God of the Ages, I pray that every flag that represents the United States would move every individual to turn toward You and to live in a way that may never disgrace it. Help each of us as citizens to reflect honor upon it. May our flag forever remain the symbol of a nation dedicated to freedom, justice, and the well-being of all mankind. Amen.

DAY 39

GENEROSITY

Americans are a generous and kindhearted people, a people who strive to strengthen and preserve those delicate bonds of affection that unite the human family and give safe harbor to all its members.

—RONALD REAGAN, FORTIETH U.S. PRESIDENT, 1989

As children of God and servants of Christ, we should be *most* generous with love. Tied to God's love are kindness, compassion, humility, and patience. These are truly "the delicate bonds" that unite the human family. Every life God creates has a beautiful and unique purpose. Being good neighbors and making positive contributions in our communities can rebuild the brokenness within our country. God created us for connection and togetherness.

"We are all parts of one body, we have the same Spirit, and we have all been called to the same glorious future" (Ephesians 4:4, TLB). God wants the same glorious future for *all* of us, not some of us. During his Fireside Chat on May 26, 1940, Franklin D. Roosevelt expressed this on behalf of the nation, stating,

> This is the promise of America. It is this that we must continue to build—this that we must continue to defend. It is the task of our generation, yours and mine. But we build and defend not for our generation alone. We defend the foundations laid down by our fathers. We build a life for generations yet unborn. We defend and we build a way of life, not for America alone, but for all mankind.

In Jesus we become one, and we're in this life together. His life was a perfect example of how we should be generous, loving one another. "Be humble and gentle. Be patient with each other, making allowance for each other's faults because of your love. Try always to be led along together by the Holy Spirit and so be at peace with one another" (Ephesians 4:2–3, TLB).

A return to the meekness of true wisdom will repair the safe harbor that is America. "*The wisdom that comes from heaven is first of all pure and full of quiet gentleness.* Then it is peace-loving and courteous. It allows discussion and is willing to yield to others; it is full of mercy and good deeds" (James 3:17, TLB, emphasis added).

Those you help will be glad not only because of your generous gifts to themselves and to others, but they will praise God for this proof that your deeds are as good as your doctrine.

—2 CORINTHIANS 9:13, TLB

REFLECT

What gifts has God given you to be generous with?

We can be generous with the fruit of the Spirit. List the fruit you might share as an act of servanthood.

What example of love during Jesus's ministry on earth inspires you most?

PRAY

Father, remove all hesitation within me to give generously as the Holy Spirit leads. Give me a heightened sense of hearing, so I can hear my shepherd's voice. Help each of us to recognize the gifts You have provided so we can be a blessing to others. Amen.

DAY 40

HOPE

Give me your tired, your poor;
Your huddled masses yearning to breathe free,
The wretched refuse of your teeming shore.
Send these, the homeless, tempest-tost to me,
I lift my lamp beside the golden door!

—*THE NEW COLOSSUS*, INSCRIBED ON A PLAQUE AT THE BASE OF THE STATUE OF LIBERTY, EMMA LAZARUS, 1883

The hope of this world, even that which is extended by our great nation, is one offered by fallible human hands. If we are to give true hope to those who come to America, we must, as one people, find it in the God who cannot fail. "Lord, let Your constant love surround us, for our hopes are in You alone" (Psalm 33:22, TLB). The poorest nations on earth can find eternal hope, and the wealthiest nations can take it for granted. If we forget the God who gave us the freedom we cherish, we forsake the only hope we have of "lifting our lamp" to the world.

"Faith is the substance of things hoped for, the evidence of things not seen" (Hebrews 11:1). Andrew Murray, a Christian pastor born in the nineteenth century said, "A revived church is the only hope for a dying world." His words ring more true today than ever. Love in action can revitalize the body of Christ, because active love is evidence of an outpouring of the Holy Spirit. "Now hope does not disappoint, because the love of God has been poured out in our hearts by the Holy Spirit who was given to us" (Romans 5:5).

While hope may be dimmed by economic barriers, growing pessimism, and political division, our eternal hope is in the Lord. Love is the greatest commandment, fastened securely to unwavering hope. The gift of the Holy Spirit will sustain us—our helper, comforter, teacher, intercessor, and friend.

Let love be without hypocrisy. Abhor what is evil. Cling to what is good. Be kindly affectionate to one another with brotherly love, in honor giving preference to one another; not lagging in diligence, fervent in spirit, serving the Lord; rejoicing in hope, patient in tribulation, continuing steadfastly in prayer.

—ROMANS 12:9–12

REFLECT

When do you feel most hopeful for the healing of our nation?

The light of our country shines brightest through love and unity. This week, what two things can you do to shine your light for others to see within your own city?

List three things you hope for as an American citizen and offer these hopes up to the Lord.

PRAY

Father, our hope is in You alone. Our nation is in need of Your love and healing. Give us the desire to renew our devotion to You—to be the lamp lifted high for the world to see. Amen.

DAY 41

JUSTICE

I now make it my earnest prayer, that God would . . . most graciously be pleased to dispose us all to do justice, to love mercy, and to demean ourselves, with that charity, humility, and pacific temper of mind, which were the characteristics of the Divine Author of our blessed religion and without a humble imitation of whose example in these things, we can never hope to be a happy Nation.

—GEORGE WASHINGTON, FOUNDER AND FIRST U.S. PRESIDENT, *CIRCULAR LETTER TO THE STATES*, 1783

It's impossible for the natural man to understand the truth of God's word. To those who haven't received the gift of salvation through Jesus Christ, truth is foolishness. As the apostle Paul wrote in his letter to Corinth, "The natural man does not receive the things of the Spirit of God, for they are foolishness to him; nor can he know them, because they are spiritually discerned" (1 Corinthians 2:14). The Holy Spirit, living within believers, opens the eyes of their understanding and magnifies the light throughout their lives. God's Spirit offers Christians the power to embody justice, mercy, and truth.

George Washington prayed earnestly that God would give the leaders of our thirteen states the temperament of the Divine Author, Jesus Christ. President Washington concluded that if we hope to be a happy nation, this is achievable only if those in authority aspire to be Christlike. *Humble*, *peaceful*, *merciful*, *charitable*, and *just* were the qualities he listed, none of which can be wholly attained by human efforts. These qualities arise within humankind through surrender to the Divine. "He has shown you, O man, what is good; And what does the Lord require of you But to do justly, To love mercy, And to walk humbly with your God?" (Micah 6:8).

The Jefferson Memorial in Washington, DC, bears these words:

> God who gave us life gave us liberty. Can the liberties of a nation be secure when we have removed a conviction that these liberties are the gift of God? Indeed I tremble for my country when I reflect that God is just, that His justice cannot sleep forever.

"Evil men do not understand justice, but those who seek the Lord understand all" (Proverbs 28:5).

The humble He guides in justice, and the humble He teaches His way. All the paths of the LORD are mercy and truth, to such as keep His covenant and His testimonies.

—PSALM 25:9–10

REFLECT

How do you define justice?

When have you witnessed someone being treated unfairly? How did you respond?

How can you support leaders who are examples of Christian principles? Write a brief prayer for our leaders.

PRAY

Father, be with those who are leading our nation, our state, and our city. Give them the courage to make decisions that align with the virtues of truth, mercy, and justice. Give them hearts of wisdom in all they do. And in all things, may You be glorified by the actions of each leader, including my family and me. Amen.

DAY 42

TRUST

I feel no great anxiety at the large armament designed against us. The remarkable interpositions of Heaven in our favor cannot be too gratefully acknowledged. He who fed the Israelites in the wilderness, who clothes the lilies of the field, and feeds the young ravens when they cry will not forsake a people engaged in so righteous a cause, if we remember His loving-kindness.

—ABIGAIL ADAMS, SECOND FIRST LADY OF THE UNITED STATES, 1776

The remarkable and miraculous involvement of God in the United States' fight for independence cannot be too gratefully acknowledged—even to this day. Our hearts should be no less sure of why we're a free and blessed nation than our founders were at its dawn. "As for God, His way is perfect; The word of the LORD is proven; He is a shield to all who trust in Him" (2 Samuel 22:31). Our absolute trust can be put in the One who deserves our profound praise and ongoing gratefulness. "Oh, bless our God, you peoples! And make the voice of His praise to be heard" (Psalm 66:8).

Abigail Adams pointed out the importance of remembering God's loving-kindness, and recounted His faithfulness since the beginning of time. She referred to the words of Jesus in Matthew 6:28–30, which reads:

> So why do you worry about clothing? Consider the lilies of the field, how they grow: they neither toil nor spin; and yet I say to you that even Solomon in all his glory was not arrayed like one of these. Now if God so clothes the grass of the field, which today is, and tomorrow is thrown into the oven, will He not much more clothe you, O you of little faith?

Charles Spurgeon, an influential nineteenth-century preacher, said, "He who truly communes with God in secret, may be trusted in public." We can trust God with the growth of our nation—but we must pray He gives us leaders who speak to Him in private.

Those who know Your name will put their trust in You; For You, LORD, have not forsaken those who seek You.

—PSALM 9:10

REFLECT

In what areas of your life is it most difficult for you to fully trust God?

Before you make choices about our elected leaders, how do you research, reflect, and listen for God's guidance?

List out your fears, questions, and struggles about the course of our nation as an act of worship and submission to the Lord.

PRAY

Father, grant us wisdom and discernment when we go to elect leaders. May we be prayerful in our decision-making and guide us to those individuals who pray—who revere and trust You with all their hearts. We put our hope in You, and seek You daily to guide our nation. Where there is unbelief, Lord, help our unbelief! Amen.

DAY 43

VISION

I am well aware of the Toil and Blood and Treasure, that it will cost Us to maintain this Declaration, and support and defend these States. —Yet through all the Gloom I can see the rays of ravishing Light and Glory. I can see that the End is more than worth all the Means.

—JOHN ADAMS, FOUNDING FATHER AND SECOND U.S. PRESIDENT, 1776

The cost of our freedom cannot be calculated. Our founders were aware of the toil, blood, and treasure that would be sacrificed to gain independence, but they couldn't have known the degree. Because they had a divinely inspired vision in their hearts and minds, they entrusted the expense to God. He revealed to them the coming light, then imbued them with the strength and wisdom to ignite it.

What a beautiful way for John Adams to describe his vision for America in a letter to his wife, Abigail, on July 3, 1776. President Adams, along with the majority of the colonists, believed the glory at the end of the sacrifice was *more* than worth all the means. Sacrifice, with a heart intent on the will of God, produces hope and light. What a poignant reminder of the path of our Savior. "For it was fitting for Him, for whom are all things and by whom are all things, in bringing many sons to glory, to make the captain of their salvation perfect through sufferings" (Hebrews 2:10).

Leaders and citizens of the thirteen colonies chose to stand as a united people, willing to risk their lives and livelihood. The signing of the U.S. Declaration of Independence took courage. This decision was proof of a deep commitment to trust God and look *ever* forward. Adams saw "rays of ravishing Light and Glory." The founding fathers maintained a vision and a hope that was anchored in faith, humility, and the fear of God.

Where there is no vision, the people perish: but he that keepeth the law, happy is he.

—PROVERBS 29:18, KJV

REFLECT

How do you ask the Holy Spirit for discernment, and how do you recognize His voice when receiving understanding?

Through prayer and Scripture, what vision has God given you—for your life and for our nation?

How do you sustain hope in challenging times?

PRAY

Father, thank You for all of the military veterans and their families. Thank You for their service and sacrifice. Bless each one with Your unending provision. Open the eyes of our nation's leaders to the truth of Your word, the light of Your salvation, and the vision of Your plan for our nation and for this world. Ignite within each military leader a passion for You and a love for peace, and lift each one as a beacon of hope held high in this darkening world. Amen.

DAY 44

PROVIDENCE

Whereas it hath pleased Almighty God, the Father of mercies, remarkably to assist and support the United States of America in their important struggle for liberty, against the long-continued efforts of a powerful nation: it is the duty of all ranks to observe and thankfully acknowledge the interpositions of his Providence in their behalf. Through the whole of this contest, from its first rise to this time, the influence of divine Providence may be clearly perceived. . . .

—OPENING LINES OF THE PROCLAMATION BY THE REVEREND JOHN WITHERSPOON FOR A DAY OF THANKSGIVING FOLLOWING THE BATTLE OF YORKTOWN, EFFECTIVELY ENDING THE AMERICAN REVOLUTION, 1781

God's hand in our nation's struggle for liberty could be clearly perceived by those who fought for it over the course of eight years—April 19, 1775, to September 3, 1783. Freedom rings today because American Patriot forces called out to God throughout the struggle. As the psalmist wrote, so the Founding Fathers believed: "Forever, O Lord, Your word is settled in heaven. Your faithfulness endures to all generations; You established the earth, and it abides" (Psalm 119:89–90). The only immutable things are those things established by God—the truth of Scripture, the way to salvation, and the nations that have been formed by His unfailing love and mercy.

In response to witnessing the "interpositions" of God, Reverend Witherspoon felt it was the duty of all Americans to *thankfully acknowledge* God's involvement in the gaining of our liberty, echoing Colossians 2:7b, "Let your lives overflow with joy and thanksgiving for all he has done" (TLB). He calls us followers of the Almighty One to lead lives that overflow with genuine thanks and true joy. These are not feelings that can be imitated or produced through worldly pursuits; they are gifts that flow from a heart surrendered to God. We have joy and gratitude to give others by God's grace alone. Our lives overflow because of Providence—the care, guidance, and protection of God.

The founders of America may have been inclined to ask the question Moses shared with Joshua while preparing him to enter the Promised Land: "I want to see the result of all the greatness and power you [Lord] have been showing us; for what God in all of heaven or earth can do what you have done for us?" (Deuteronomy 3:25, TLB).

Oh, let the nations be glad and sing for joy!
For You shall judge the people righteously,
And govern the nations on earth.

PSALM 67:4

REFLECT

In contemplation, how does the faithful care of God inspire thankfulness in you?

How do you see Providence—"divine guidance or care" as defined by Merriam-Webster—in the news today? What might you do to point out God's power and sustaining guidance in your city?

A life that overflows with joy is only possible in a life that teems with gratitude. What habits have you formed, knowing joy and thanksgiving go hand in hand?

PRAY

Father, thank You for being powerfully present when freedom was established in the United States. Restore to us the joy of Your salvation, and give us hearts that want to obey You. Help us to be aware of Your divine presence, offering up our words, our conversations, our lives, and this nation into Your almighty hands. Amen.

DAY 45

SACRIFICE

I love the religion of our blessed Savior! I love that religion that comes from above. I love that religion that sends its votaries [followers] to bind up the wounds of him that has fallen among thieves. I love that religion that makes it the duty of its disciples to visit the fatherless and the widow in their affliction. I love that religion that is based upon the glorious principle of love to God and love to man—which makes its followers do unto others as they themselves would be done by.

—FREDERICK DOUGLASS, FORMER SLAVE, MINISTER, AND ABOLITIONIST, 1846

The spiritually sound principles of loving God and loving mankind built our nation. These pillars are the greatest commandments God has given us, and the greatest threat to our nation is allowing them to crumble. "Walk in love, as Christ also has loved us and given Himself for us, an offering and a sacrifice to God for a sweet-smelling aroma" (Ephesians 5:2). Walking in love doesn't mean we agree on everything. Love isn't elevated by winning arguments. Love is exalted by the truth of God's word. Love prevails when compassion persists. Love defines those who value humility, generosity, and joy. "The sacrifices of God are a broken spirit, A broken and contrite heart—These, O God, You will not despise" (Psalm 51:17).

Frederick Douglass witnessed unimaginable suffering in the early years of his life. He was sold into slavery at six years old. But love had a plan for him before he was born. God chose him, called him, and carried him out of the darkness and into His marvelous light. Douglass fell in love with the Savior of the world, and love guided him to God's purpose. He was laser-focused on the power of love to change the course of a life and resuscitate the life of a nation.

> They cried out to the Lord in their trouble, and He saved them out of their distresses. He sent His word and healed them, and delivered them from their destructions. Oh, that men would give thanks to the Lord for His goodness and for His wonderful works to the children of men! Let them sacrifice the sacrifices of thanksgiving, and declare His works with rejoicing. (Psalm 107:19–22)

I beseech you therefore, brethren, by the mercies of God, that you present your bodies a living sacrifice, holy, acceptable to God, which is your reasonable service. And do not be conformed to this world, but be transformed by the renewing of your mind, that you may prove what is that good and acceptable and perfect will of God.

—ROMANS 12:1–2

REFLECT

How have you expressed God's love in a dark world this week?

What has been the strongest evidence of God's love as an active force in your life?

In what ways do you feel inspired to extend God's love to others? What gifts does the Holy Spirit lead you to share?

PRAY

Father, have mercy on us. Forgive us for those times when Your love was not a priority. Rain down Your love and change us from the inside out. May Your Spirit sweep over this country like never before. Help us to see our neighbors as brothers and sisters, created in Your image, and to esteem the value of life as children of Your grace. Amen.

DAY 46

ROSE

Americans have always loved the flowers with which God decorates our land. More often than any other flower, we hold the rose dear as the symbol of life and love and devotion, of beauty and eternity. For the love of man and woman, for the love of mankind and God, for the love of country, Americans who would speak the language of the heart do so with a rose. The American people have long held a special place in their hearts for roses. Let us continue to cherish them, to honor the love and devotion they represent, and to bestow them on all we love just as God has bestowed them on us.

—RONALD REAGAN, FORTIETH U.S. PRESIDENT, DECLARING THE ROSE AS THE NATIONAL FLORAL EMBLEM OF THE UNITED STATES, 1986

Our first president, George Washington, was the first rose breeder in the United States. He hybridized a rose and named it after his mother, the "Mary Washington" rose. It's an old garden variety known for its large, fragrant blooms. The rose is one of the oldest flowers, is edible and rich in Vitamin C, is notable for its range of fragrances, and is often used in perfumes.

In 1986, the rose became the floral emblem of the United States. As Ronald Reagan put it, we are a *God-decorated* land, a country vast in natural beauty and abundant resources. It's fitting that a flower representative of honor, love, and devotion be named as our floral emblem—they are all things we attribute to God, our Creator. "All day long I'll praise and honor you, O God, for all that you have done for me" (Psalm 71:8, TLB).

A twentieth-century President echoed the sentiment of our founding fathers. "Let those who love Your salvation exclaim, 'What a wonderful God he is!' " (Psalm 70:4, TLB). This admission is the definitive reason our nation's prosperity endures. "The grass withers, the flowers fade, but the word of our God shall stand forever" (Isaiah 40:8, TLB). This nation's provision is in a faithful God, our hope is in the Lord's salvation, and *both* encourage our devotion to God. His love and His word are eternal. When God is the rejoicing of our hearts, blessing will be the response of His.

If God cares so wonderfully for flowers that are here today and gone tomorrow, won't he more surely care for you?

—MATTHEW 6:30, TLB

REFLECT

What part of God's creation inspires you the most?

Where do you feel close to God when you spend time in the natural world?

How are you deliberate about spending time outdoors or meditating on God's creation?

PRAY

Father, I'm thankful for the beauty You created for us to enjoy. I praise You for the amazing landscape of our land. Help me notice the miracles and the majesty in nature. Thank you that so many U.S. leaders have set aside protected parks and land across the nation, our state, and even in our city. Please help us to be good stewards of the resources You have created, honoring Your handiwork. Protect and give wisdom to those who work for park services across our nation. Amen.

DAKOTA TY.
NEBRASKA
KANSAS
COLORADO
WYOMING
UTAH
ARIZONA TY.
NEW MEXICO TY.
TEXAS
ARKANSAS
KENTUCKY
TENNESSEE
OHIO
WISCONSIN
GULF OF MEXICO

DAY 47

HUMILITY

I shall look for whatever success may attend my public service; and knowing that "except the Lord keep the city the watchman waketh but in vain," with fervent supplications for His favor, to His overruling providence I commit with humble but fearless confidence my own fate and the future destinies of my country.

—JOHN QUINCY ADAMS, SIXTH U.S. PRESIDENT, INAUGURAL ADDRESS, 1825

Power with humility is the only true path to blessing for our nation. "By humility and the fear of the LORD are riches and honor and life" (Proverbs 22:4). The journey of our country has taken us through times of war, the sins of slavery, the struggle for equality, and the dangers of division. We would not remain in existence without the grace of God. The return to humility—from the top of our government to our local leaders to individual citizens—is imperative for America's survival and success.

Let us have ears to hear the words of Paul:

> Therefore, as the elect of God, holy and beloved, put on tender mercies, kindness, humility, meekness, longsuffering, bearing with one another, and forgiving one another, if anyone has a complaint against another; even as Christ forgave you, so you also must do. But above all these things put on love, which is the bond of perfection. (Colossians 3:12–14)

John Quincy Adams, sixth president of the U.S., quoted from Psalm 127:1, "Unless the LORD builds the house, they labor in vain who build it; unless the LORD guards the city, the watchman stays awake in vain." With a single verse of truth, he laid down his term, his efforts, and his success to the will of God, beneath the covering of prayer. With "humble but fearless confidence" he surrendered his fate and the destiny of our country. We need leaders with hearts for God. It is our highest hope for our brightest future. As we humble ourselves before God in prayer, we invite the Spirit of God to heal us.

The Lord is good and glad to teach the proper path to all who go astray; he will teach the ways that are right and best to those who humbly turn to him. And when we obey him, every path he guides us on is fragrant with his loving-kindness and his truth.

—PSALM 25:8–10, TLB

REFLECT

Why do you think individuals resist being humble?

When electing leaders who are humble, what do you look for?

What do you do in your own life to keep humility and love above all?

PRAY

Father, give us leaders who walk in humility and surrender. Show them the ways of wisdom, compassion, and love. Allow strength to come from being a servant. Create in each of us a clean heart and help us to look at the heart rather than the exterior of those around us. Reveal to me and to elected officials the steps toward fearless confidence in You alone. Amen.

DAY 48

SERVICE

I do solemnly swear that I will support and defend the Constitution of the United States against all enemies, foreign and domestic; that I will bear true faith and allegiance to the same; and that I will obey the orders of the President of the United States and the orders of the officers appointed over me, according to regulations and the Uniform Code of Military Justice. So help me God.

—U.S. MILITARY OATH OF ENLISTMENT

Service for the honor of the U.S. Constitution and country begins with reverence for something greater than ourselves. Men and women choose to enlist in the U.S. military branches every day for personal reasons, many of which answer the call to serve the American people and the greater good of peace around the globe. Each of us is called to serve. Jesus was the ultimate model of service. In Matthew 20:25–28 Jesus says,

> You know that the rulers of the Gentiles lord it over them, and those who are great exercise authority over them. Yet it shall not be so among you; but whoever desires to become great among you, let him be your servant. And whoever desires to be first among you, let him be your slave—just as the Son of Man did not come to be served, but to serve, and to give His life a ransom for many.

Without a sincere love for God, humans are not able to cultivate a true love for others and take on the role of servant. "For, dear brothers, you have been given freedom: not freedom to do wrong, but freedom to love and serve each other" (Galatians 5:13, TLB).

Wholeheartedly serving others binds itself to serving God. Apart, we strive in our own strength, sin in our selfish nature, and struggle in our separation from truth. "My eyes shall be on the faithful of the land, that they may dwell with me; he who walks in a perfect way, he shall serve me" (Psalm 101:6). The security and defense of our country are in the salvation of our Lord. "Let all those rejoice who put their trust in You; Let them ever shout for joy, because You defend them; Let those also who love Your name be joyful in You" (Psalm 5:11).

The Oath of Enlistment to serve in our military concludes with a plea for God's help—precisely where our help rests. "I will lift up my eyes to the hills—from whence comes my help? My help comes from the LORD, who made heaven and earth" (Psalm 121:1–2). There is no cry unanswered when it falls on God's ears. He is our Father, He is for us, and He is faithful.

He who loves his life will lose it, and he who hates his life in this world will keep it for eternal life. If anyone serves Me, let him follow Me; and where I am, there My servant will be also. If anyone serves Me, him My Father will honor.

—JOHN 12:25–26

REFLECT

How do you serve in your city?

How can you help in areas where the gospel is not routinely heard?

How has the Holy Spirit led you to pray for the law enforcement and first responders in your city?

PRAY

Father, I lift to You those who serve our community and our country. Protect those who are on the frontlines in our cities, states, borders, and military bases. Give each person who serves strength both mentally and physically to do the work You've called them to. Spread peace that passes understanding in areas that face turmoil and upheaval. Open our eyes to ways we can serve each day in the places we walk and with the people we encounter. Amen.

DAY 49

PROMISE

It is a clear and just thing, and my God that has given it [the charter for the land in America that would become Pennsylvania] to me through many difficulties, will, I believe, bless and make it the seed of a nation.

—WILLIAM PENN, FOUNDER OF PENNSYLVANIA, 1681

We serve a God who keeps His promises. He revealed the promise of a nation to the hearts of its founders, and subsequently, to those who would carry the torch forward. From humble beginnings, we hold to the proclamation *In God we trust*. He's the only One who faithfully fulfills every word He's spoken. Many people come to the United States seeking the promise of a better life—a job, education for their children, safety, and freedom to worship. America still holds promise just as the founding fathers had envisioned.

When 37-year-old William Penn was granted the charter for Pennsylvania by King Charles II nearly 100 years before the Revolutionary War began, Penn took on the responsibility with a firm grasp of God's grace and provision. Penn told his constituents, "You shall be governed by laws of your own making and live a free, and if you will, a sober and industrious life. I shall not usurp the right of any, or oppress his person. God has furnished me with a better resolution and has given me His grace to keep it. . . . "

The "better resolution" Penn might have alluded to likely included the inalienable rights of every person—as written in our Declaration of Independence more than 100 years later. Penn noted that he would not oppress or usurp the rights of any person, and would achieve that promise by God's grace. The wisdom of that statement reveals the state of Penn's heart. When we make a promise to commit to God the work we're given, He promises to give us what we need to accomplish it. "Be of good courage, and He shall strengthen your heart, all you who hope in the LORD" (Psalm 31:24).

The Lord is not slack concerning His promise, as some count slackness, but is longsuffering toward us, not willing that any should perish but that all should come to repentance.

—2 PETER 3:9

REFLECT

What do you think William Penn meant when he said, "God has furnished me with a better resolution" for the leadership role he was given?

List out a few of God's promises noted in Scripture.

What promises have you seen fulfilled for America by the grace of God?

PRAY

Father, thank You for promising eternal life to those who believe in Jesus. Thank You for allowing the United States of America to hold promise for its citizens and many others around the world. Help us not to take this for granted. In Your mercy, Lord, provide the governors of the 50 states wisdom to lead with Your love and grace. Strengthen them to do their jobs with courage and compassion. Amen.

with a firm reliance on the protection of
John Hancock
Samuel Chase
Wm. Paca
Thos. Stone
John Morton
Jas. Smith
Geo. Taylor
James Wilson
George Wythe
Richard Henry Lee
Caesar Rodney

HONOR

And for the support of this Declaration, with a firm reliance on the protection of divine Providence we mutually pledge to each other our Lives, our Fortunes, and our sacred Honor.

—CONCLUSION OF THE DECLARATION OF INDEPENDENCE, JULY 4, 1776

The fifty-six men who signed the U.S. Declaration of Independence mutually pledged to each other their sacred honor. They committed themselves to maintaining a deep and mutual respect, while holding one another in high esteem. How vastly differently we see our leaders regarding one another today. In response, let us pray that the humility of our founding fathers might permeate the hearts and minds of the men and women in positions of authority today. God rewards those who follow His way. "Work hard and cheerfully at all you do, just as though you were working for the Lord and not merely for your masters" (Colossians 3:23, TLB).

President Calvin Coolidge was quoted as saying, "No person was ever honored for what he received. Honor has been the reward for what he gave." This statement came nearly 150 years after the Declaration of Independence and echoes Proverbs 29:23, "A man's pride will bring him low, But the humble in spirit will retain honor."

Hearts that are teachable are receptive to the leading of the Holy Spirit. There could be no wider path to a blessed nation than to fill our government with leaders who honor God. Praying for men and women who seek His wisdom—from town halls and school boards, to governors' mansions, to the Capitol, and to the White House—should be a pressing mandate for everyone who loves this country. God will meet our requests with mercy. "You meet him who rejoices and does righteousness, who remembers You in Your ways" (Isaiah 64:5a).

Loving God leads to godly desires, which ultimately guide us into His good and perfect will. When the founders declared freedom in 1776, they understood that independence would be won only with the help of God. Our unity will be revived in this same manner. "For Christ himself is our way of peace. He has made peace between us . . . breaking down the wall of contempt that used to separate us" (Ephesians 2:14, TLB).

Glory and honor to God forever and ever. He is the King of the ages, the unseen one who never dies; he alone is God, and full of wisdom. Amen.

—1 TIMOTHY 1:17, TLB

REFLECT

How has the Holy Spirit directed you to pray for our country and its leaders even when you disagree with their decisions?

In honoring those in authority, how do you refrain from speaking negatively and instead speak words that honor God and reveal His love?

Romans 12:10 says, "Be kindly affectionate to one another with brotherly love, in honor giving preference to one another." Why do you think God has given His followers this commandment?

PRAY

Father, shower Your perfect love on those in authority. Remove any blinders the enemy has used to keep our leaders from seeing Your goodness and grace. Pour out Your healing oil of the Holy Spirit on our country, from the highest positions to those in our cities and neighborhoods. Anoint our lips with words of peace and honor. Amen.

DAY 51

STRENGTH

So it was with me. I had crossed the line of which I had so long been dreaming. I was free; but there was no one to welcome me to the land of freedom, I was a stranger in a strange land. . . . But to this solemn resolution I came; I was free, and they [my family] should be free also; I would make a home for them in the North, and the Lord helping me I would bring them all there. Oh, how I prayed then, lying all alone on the cold damp ground; "Oh, dear Lord," I said, "I ain't got no friend but You. Come to my help, Lord, for I'm in trouble!"

—HARRIET TUBMAN, FORMER SLAVE AND ABOLITIONIST, 1849

★ ★ ★ ★ ★

The quiet prayers only God hears are as powerful as any supplication shouted from a stage. We can feel Harriet Tubman's heart beating with a hope she dared to embrace, in the God who would not fail her. We cannot imagine the pain or struggle she endured as a slave, but we can intimately know the God she cried out to. He is still the hope of every heart. He is still our light in suffocating darkness. He is still the love that can reshape the world and restore a nation. And above all, He is our strength.

When we pray with the determination of a people desperate for more of our Savior's mercy and love, we invite God's presence into our longing. It seems hard to understand and harder to do, but the truth is ours to believe: "Do not sorrow, for the joy of the LORD is your strength" (Nehemiah 8:10b). The only way to find joy in the depth of tribulation is to cry out to God. As our nation struggles to be united, God will meet us with an answer. We are strengthened by the power of His love through kindness, service, and mutual respect. Our nation is strongest when we stand together. Division weakens our ability to communicate, connect, and exude compassion. A conscious decision to stay focused on the source of our strength, rather than the distance of our differences, will lift us out of the chasm that separates us. America is one nation under God, and we draw closer to that truth by drawing closer to Him.

Have you not known? Have you not heard? The everlasting God, the LORD, The Creator of the ends of the earth, Neither faints nor is weary. His understanding is unsearchable. He gives power to the weak, And to those who have no might He increases strength.

—ISAIAH 40:28–29

REFLECT

How do you restore your strength during a trial?

Read Isaiah 40:31. How might you pray for God to strengthen our elected leaders?

Jesus said to the apostle Paul in 2 Corinthians 12:9, “My strength is made perfect in weakness.” In what areas of your life do you need the Lord’s strength to prevail?

PRAY

Father, thank You for listening when we cry out to You. The strength You give through the power of the Holy Spirit keeps us going. Fill us with joy as we persevere through difficult times in our nation, and when we are weak, Lord, may Your strength guide us forward. Hold us closely in our times of need. Amen.

DAY 52

PROTECT

O Trinity of love and power!
Our brethren shield in danger's hour;
From rock and tempest, fire and foe,
Protect them wheresoe'er they go;
Thus evermore shall rise to Thee
Glad hymns of praise from land and sea.

—WILLIAM WHITING, FINAL VERSE OF
THE UNITED STATES NAVY HYMN, 1860

God is our shelter, our refuge, and our rock. The utterance of His word is the sword of the Spirit—a weapon we should wield every day. Speaking the word of God sets His angels to task. Psalm 103:20 says, "Bless the Lord, you His angels, Who excel in strength, who do His word, Heeding the voice of His word." When we give God's word *sound*, He hears our cry and instructs. The angels carry out His decree and take action.

From the early governing of our nation, Divine protection was sought after and witnessed. In 1787, Benjamin Franklin called for the Constitutional Convention to begin its deliberations with prayer. He said, "I have lived a long time and the longer I live, the more convincing proofs I see of this truth—that God governs in the affairs of men. And if a sparrow cannot fall without His notice, is it probable that an empire can rise without His aid?" He also stated, "In the beginning of the contest with Britain, when we were sensible of danger, we had daily prayers in this room for Divine protection. Our prayers were heard, and they were graciously answered. . . . Do we imagine we no longer need His assistance?"

Our prayers can still be lifted as we start our days—as citizens, leaders, and the body of Christ: "Hear my cry, O God; attend to my prayer. From the end of the earth I will cry to You, When my heart is overwhelmed; Lead me to the rock that is higher than I. For You have been a shelter for me, a strong tower from the enemy" (Psalm 61:1–3).

He who dwells in the secret place of the Most High
Shall abide under the shadow of the Almighty.
I will say of the LORD, "He is my refuge and my fortress; My God, in Him I will trust."

—PSALM 91:1–2

REFLECT

"The name of the Lord *is* a strong tower; The righteous run to it and are safe" (Proverbs 18:10). What does this verse mean to you?

What Scriptures guide you as you pray for God's protection over your family?

How might you pray for God's protection over our leaders and over national security threats, military deployments, and foreign influence?

PRAY

Father, shed Your light on our nation, and keep us from straying away from the truth of Your word. Help our leaders lift their eyes to You, and give them courage every day. Have mercy upon us as our nation seeks to have a positive influence around the globe. Help us to keep Your name at the forefront of our minds. Amen.

DAY 53

PURSUIT OF HAPPINESS

I have lived to see a great work accomplished, yet much still remains to be done to secure the happiness of this Country. May that Almighty Being who has thus far conducted us safely through many scenes of difficulty and distress inspire the people of these United States with wisdom to improve the opportunity now afforded of becoming a happy nation.

—CHARLES THOMSON, SECRETARY OF THE CONTINENTAL CONGRESS, 1784

The pursuit of happiness is our inalienable right; and a truly blessed life filled with peace, contentment, and self-control cannot be separated from a right relationship with God through Jesus. The former is solely dependent on the latter. We hear this echoed in the words of Thomas Jefferson, who said, "The doctrines of Jesus are simple, and tend all to the happiness of man."

Put another way, the pursuit of happiness is the path to Jesus. He is where true fulfillment begins. Genuine enrichment comes by cultivating a life of virtue and moral excellence. This pursuit can't be attained without our Savior. Those who founded America connected the pursuit of happiness to the "law of nature and of nature's God." This inalienable right is not a hedonistic quest for pleasure, but a civic and personal obligation to live a virtuous and flourishing life based on rational decisions.

The commandments we're given in Mark 12:29–31 are simple to understand but take discipline to follow. "'The Lord our God is the one and only God. And you must love him with all your heart and soul and mind and strength.' The second is: 'You must love others as much as yourself.' No other commandments are greater than these" (TLB). Love is a decision followed by a commitment. It's an act of obedience to God, and obedience brings good outcomes. If we hope to harvest unity as a country, we have to pursue love as individuals. Our daily goals should include being an active part of bringing God's love into the world. Our lives are blessed when we look outward to the needs of our neighbors instead of inward to the selfishness of our flesh. "It is possible to give away and become richer! It is also possible to hold on too tightly and lose everything" (Proverbs 11:24, TLB).

Delight yourself also in the LORD,
And He shall give you the desires of your heart.

—PSALM 37:4

REFLECT

What does happiness mean to you?

To what extent does society's definition of happiness conflict with the Bible's definition of happiness?

What are the benefits and drawbacks for our nation as individuals pursue happiness today?

PRAY

Father, may we be called to a higher standard of happiness as a nation. Help us to seek the type of joy You can provide. Transform our nation, allowing us to nurture a habitation for happiness You define. Open our minds and hearts to give freely to others. Open our eyes and our ears to ways we can support the weak and the vulnerable. Amen.

DAY 54

VICTORY

The highest glory of the American Revolution was this: it connected in one indissoluble bond the principles of civil government with the principles of Christianity.

—JOHN QUINCY ADAMS, SIXTH U.S. PRESIDENT, JULY 4, 1821

Our nation is in a spiritual battle. Our prayers are the way to certain victory. The power is ours to use, and the instructions from the apostle Paul are clear:

> Be strong in the Lord and in the power of His might. Put on the whole armor of God, that you may be able to stand against the wiles of the devil. For we do not wrestle against flesh and blood, but against principalities, against powers, against the rulers of the darkness of this age, against spiritual hosts of wickedness in the heavenly places. Therefore take up the whole armor of God, that you may be able to withstand in the evil day, and having done all, to stand. (Ephesians 6:10–13)

John Quincy Adams made an inspired observation when he said that the *highest glory* of winning our independence was the inseparable bond of the principles of our government with the principles of Christianity. If we as a people allow the two to be divided, we risk seeing the glory of our great nation destroyed. "Where there is ignorance of God, crime runs wild; but what a wonderful thing it is for a nation to know and keep his laws" (Proverbs 29:18, TLB).

The victory of our country depends on the voice of our people. It's a critical time for us to stand on truth while kneeling in humility—and we can be fearless in following through. "For I, the Lord your God, will hold your right hand, saying to you, 'Fear not, I will help you'" (Isaiah 41:13).

Thanks be to God, who gives us the victory through our Lord Jesus Christ. Therefore . . . be steadfast, immovable, always abounding in the work of the Lord, knowing that your labor is not in vain in the Lord.

—1 CORINTHIANS 15:57–58

REFLECT

How has the Holy Spirit helped you with overcoming fear in these difficult times?

How does this passage invoke a victory mindset for you?

> For the Lord says, "Because he loves me, I will rescue him; I will make him great because he trusts in my name. When he calls on me, I will answer; I will be with him in trouble and rescue him and honor him. I will satisfy him with a full life and give him my salvation." (Psalm 91:14–16, TLB)

In what ways would you like to see God's victory sweep across America?

PRAY

Father, with You, we know the battle is won. Give us strength, wisdom, and hope as we seek You continually, as one people and one nation. Refresh our minds with the truth of Your power. Enliven our hearts with a courageous spirit to live in victory. Amen.

E PLURIBUS UNUM.

DAY 55

UNITY

E PLURIBUS UNUM, meaning "Out of many, one."

—ENGRAVED ON THE GALLERY IN THE
HOUSE OF REPRESENTATIVES
CHAMBER OF THE U.S. CAPITOL BUILDING

There is strength in unity, and God is the source of both. Today, as part of our hard-fought freedom, we are many cultures and many beliefs—but we must remain one nation under God. The God we serve gave His Son for every person on earth. We are loved and valued equally by our Creator. Love is the binding agent. Honoring the worth of every human life invites the love of God to thrive among us. Love is the one thing that will benefit the good of *every* person and *every* hope our nation aspires to. We cannot hate and hope to survive.

The words engraved in the House Chamber of our Capitol Building beg to stir our remembrance of the power of being *one people*. It doesn't imply we are the same. Each of us is as unique as the purpose God designed us to fulfill. But *out of many*—the many different lives, experiences, cultures, and beliefs—we are *one* in our humanity. Love doesn't discriminate, demean, or devalue. Love sees, has sympathy, and serves. Love holds the power to pull our nation together.

A spirit of unity can only flow from the hearts of our leaders if they humble themselves. Humility allows God access to a willing vessel, one He can pour into, one in which mercy and goodness bless the nation. When we lift up those who govern us in prayer and intercede for them through the lens of love and compassion, God hears and answers.

[Jesus said,] "My prayer for all of them is that they will be of one heart and mind, just as you and I are, Father—that just as you are in me and I am in you, so they will be in us, and the world will believe you sent me."

—JOHN 17:21, TLB

REFLECT

What shared American values can unite people across deep political and ideological divides?

What areas do you feel are most in need of unity when you reflect on the state of our nation?

Love is the unifying force for all that is good. How will you put love in action this week?

PRAY

Father, let the prayer of our Savior be revived in us, that we may know "the glorious unity of being one"—as the body of Christ and a nation surrendered to You. Bring reconciliation to our land. Release Your Spirit and invigorate harmony in all communities. Heal broken relationships. Forgive past sins. And help us to see brothers and sisters rather than differences and division. Amen.

DAY 56

PEACE

We cannot better express ourselves than by humbly supplicating the Supreme Ruler of the world that the rod of tyrants may be broken to pieces, and the oppressed made free again: that wars may cease in all the earth, and that the confusions that are and have been among nations may be overruled by promoting and speedily bringing on that holy and happy period when the kingdom of our Lord and Savior Jesus Christ may be everywhere established, and all people everywhere willingly bow to the scepter of Him who is Prince of Peace.

—SAMUEL ADAMS, FOUNDER AND GOVERNOR OF MASSACHUSETTS, 1797

Peace is a product of heaven brought to us by the Savior of this world. When Samuel Adams looked forward to "that holy and happy period when the kingdom of our Lord and Savior Jesus Christ may be everywhere established," he could not know the timing, nor can we. It is for God alone to know, and His timing is as perfect as His love.

The peace we can maintain while on earth is fully dependent on the One who created our world and everything in it. It is a spiritual blessing that is internally kept and externally unaffected. "You will keep him in perfect peace, Whose mind is stayed on You, Because he trusts in You" (Isaiah 26:3). We have peace with God through Jesus, and nothing is more calming. It's characterized by self-control, a fruit of the Spirit, and it is visible in our countenance.

Peace in the midst of confusion and chaos is contagious—and it points people to our Savior. God knew we'd see dark and difficult days in our country. "Those who decide to please Christ Jesus by living godly lives will suffer at the hands of those who hate him" (2 Timothy 3:12, TLB). God also knows the power of His word and the promise of His presence is all we need to withstand and defeat whatever comes against us. "The Lord will give strength to His people; The Lord will bless His people with peace" (Psalm 29:11).

These things I have spoken to you, that in Me you may have peace. In the world you will have tribulation; but be of good cheer, I have overcome the world.

—JOHN 16:33

REFLECT

When do you feel most at peace?

How do personal values and experiences shape our society's understanding of peace and our efforts to achieve it?

In the midst of a trial how have you experienced "peace that passes understanding" (Philippians 4:7)?

PRAY

Father, give us Your peace. Give us the confidence and calm that come through the peace we have in Jesus. When tribulation comes to our nation or our families, strengthen our resolve in knowing we can rejoice because You have overcome this world. Amen.

DAY 57

FAITHFUL

Semper Fidelis, meaning "Always Faithful."

—MOTTO OF THE UNITED STATES MARINE CORPS

"The secret strength of a nation is found in the faith that abides in the hearts and the homes of the country." That truth was spoken by American pastor Billy Graham. When we stand together as a people, faithful to the God who has held us together from the beginning, we are stronger than we know and more blessed than we can imagine. Jesus said in John 20:29, "Blessed are those who have not seen and yet have believed."

God has not turned His back on our nation, nor will He if we continue to call on His name. "Fear not, for I am with you; Be not dismayed, for I am your God. I will strengthen you, Yes, I will help you, I will uphold you with My righteous right hand" (Isaiah 41:10). His right hand will not fail us when the righteous in Christ are among us. We have a faithful God whose purposes will prevail in spite of challenges, circumstances, and continued assaults on the truth. He has created us, and He is well able to keep us.

The motto of the United States Marine Corps is beholden to the One who is *eternally* faithful. Without God, we cannot hope to uphold the promises made in our human strength. We can depend on Him to be ever faithful in helping us overcome. We can put our complete trust in Him to see us through every battle we face, as followers of Christ and a nation in His care. "Don't be afraid . . . for the Lord your God will fight for you" (Deuteronomy 3:22, TLB).

Know that the LORD your God, He is God, the faithful God who keeps covenant and mercy for a thousand generations with those who love Him and keep His commandments.

—DEUTERONOMY 7:9

REFLECT

What are the most pivotal times you've experienced the faithfulness of God in your life?

In what areas are you asking God to be faithful to our nation?

How are you praying for God to reveal His faithfulness to your family right now?

PRAY

Father, we stand in awe of Your continued faithfulness to our country even when we have strayed from its founding principles. Move the hearts of our citizens to live with faith, compassion, and kindness, fostering unity and understanding in our diverse society. With humility and repentance, we ask for Your mercy to cover us now and in the future. Amen.

DAY 58

GRATITUDE

God of our fathers, whose almighty hand
Leads forth in beauty all the starry bands
Of shining worlds in splendor through the skies,
Our grateful songs before thy throne arise.

—DANIEL CRANE ROBERTS, "GOD OF OUR FATHERS"
(OFTEN CALLED THE NATIONAL HYMN), 1876

Daniel Crane Roberts served in the American Civil War with the 84th Ohio Volunteers. He wrote "God of Our Fathers" for a small-town celebration when our nation was preparing to celebrate the 100th anniversary of the Declaration of Independence. It was a song of gratitude for God's almighty hand at work in the birth and growth of our nation. The lyric of his hymn holds true, as our gratefulness rises to God with a renewed passion. "Lord, with all my heart I thank you. I will sing your praises before the armies of angels" (Psalm 138:1, TLB).

Gratitude is the way we go forward into all God has for us. The United States of America is lifted by God's hand alone, for His glory alone. Gratefulness is the soil of humility, allowing it to grow and produce a people that glorifies God through unity, compassion, and love. It's time for us to see each other the way God sees each one of us: "You are precious to me and honored, and I love you" (Isaiah 43:4, TLB). Our lives depend on accepting what God has done for us. "God showed how much he loved us by sending his only Son into this wicked world to bring to us eternal life through his death" (1 John 4:9, TLB).

Gratitude and love will see us through, grace will carry us through, and God will pull us through. Whatever challenges lie ahead, God has already met—and He can be trusted with them all. "His name shall endure forever; His name shall continue as long as the sun. And men shall be blessed in Him; All nations shall call Him blessed" (Psalm 72:17).

Oh, how grateful and thankful I am to the Lord because he is so good. I will sing praise to the name of the Lord who is above all lords.

—PSALM 7:17, TLB

REFLECT

Who is one person who helped shape you into the person you are today, and what would you thank them for?

In what ways has your gratefulness grown for all God has done in your life this past year?

What is something unexpected that you are grateful for today?

PRAY

Father, my soul is filled with gratitude for all You've done. I put my hope in You for the future of our nation. I trust in Your wisdom and lean on Your strength. I praise You for Your faithfulness. Help me to be a blessing to those around my neighborhood and city. Amen.

DAY 59

TRANQUILITY

Our fathers' God, to Thee,
Author of liberty,
To Thee we sing.
Long may our land be bright
With freedom's holy light;
Protect us by Thy might,
Great God, our King!

—SAMUEL F. SMITH, FOURTH VERSE OF
"MY COUNTRY, 'TIS OF THEE," 1831

Author of liberty. The One who authored our liberty by giving our founders the strength to secure it is the same One who secured our salvation. Our praise and prayers enter the throne room where He now sits—watching and interceding without pause. "Looking unto Jesus, the author and finisher of our faith, who for the joy that was set before Him endured the cross, despising the shame, and has sat down at the right hand of the throne of God" (Hebrews 12:2). Nineteenth-century South African pastor Andrew Murray inspires us to spend time there with these words, "Oh, let the place of secret prayer become to me the most beloved spot on earth."

The presence of God is where true tranquility resides. With Him, there's a peace that goes beyond what we can foster on our own. "The peace of God, which surpasses all understanding, will guard your hearts and minds through Christ Jesus" (Philippians 4:7). This world is our current residence, but through stillness, quietness, and prayer, we can spend time with our coming King.

Freedom's holy light. Do we remember our freedom is sacred? The One who made us free is worthy of our reverence, respect, and *all* of our praise. The freedoms our nation has been given shine a light in this earth—a holy beacon powered by God for the purpose of spreading His love. With His call to America comes a responsibility for its citizens. When we exalt Him, humanity finds their way—and finds their eternal hope. "And I, if I am lifted up from the earth, will draw all peoples to Myself" (John 12:32).

Let the heavens rejoice, and let the earth be glad;
And let them say among the nations,
"The LORD reigns."

—1 CHRONICLES 16:31

REFLECT

What small adjustments can you make in your daily routine to be still before God?

What conditions in society might hinder or promote widespread peace?

In what ways do you believe God has established the United States to be a light in the world?

PRAY

Father, You are the author of peace. Give us, as one people exalting You, a deeper desire to spend time in prayer and praise so we can be vessels of tranquility. Allow America to be a beacon spreading peace and light, so Your name is glorified. Amen.

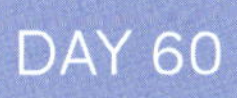

HOME

God bless America,
Land that I love.
Stand beside her, and guide her
Thru the night with the light from above.
From the mountains, to the prairies,
To the oceans, white with foam
God bless America, My home sweet home.

—IRVING BERLIN, "GOD BLESS AMERICA," 1918

The words "God bless America" are often the conclusion of speeches made in the U.S. We expect to hear it and carry on without giving much thought about it. But we should *never* stop thinking about it or take this phrase for granted. Do we truly want God's blessing on our country? Do we honestly seek His blessing on our leaders, neighbors, families, and children? God told Abram, who would become Abraham, "Don't be fearful . . . for I will defend you. And I will give you great blessings" (Genesis 15:1, TLB). God will not break the promise He made, and in Christ Jesus, that promise is ours. The apostle Paul encourages us, "If you are Christ's, then you are Abraham's seed, and heirs according to the promise" (Galatians 3:29).

Salvation moves us from thinking we know what's best to being certain only God knows what is best. The willing sacrifice Jesus made for our stubborn, rebellious souls takes us from being eternally separated from God to the unimaginable peace and privilege of spending eternity in His presence. He is our *true* home. "For our citizenship is in heaven, from which we also eagerly wait for the Savior, the Lord Jesus Christ" (Philippians 3:20).

Our time on earth could not be spent in a more beautiful place—from our mountains, to our prairies, to the oceans of our coasts. We are a free nation because God has chosen to bless us. And because grace came through the life of our Savior, He has not left us. "Peace I leave with you, My peace I give to you; not as the world gives do I give to you. Let not your heart be troubled, neither let it be afraid" (John 14:27).

For we know that when this tent we live in now is taken down—when we die and leave these bodies—we will have wonderful new bodies in heaven, homes that will be ours forevermore, made for us by God himself and not by human hands.

—2 CORINTHIANS 5:1, TLB

REFLECT

What does the idea of home mean to you?

List three reasons you're thankful to call America home.

What encourages you about the promise of a heavenly home?

PRAY

Father, I praise and thank You for the United States of America. Thank you for the gift of shelter. I pray this homeland would become a place of strength, restoration, and unity. We call on You to make Your home in America. We welcome the Holy Spirit to this dwelling place and dedicate this nation to Your will. Transform our hearts and strengthen the bonds between us for good. Amen.

ABOUT THE AUTHOR

Bonnie Rickner Jensen grew up with a father and mother who loved God and modeled His grace to their six children. She thinks of her dad as a "car ride" preacher who spent the countless road trips of her childhood teaching his children the truth of God's Word. She gave her life to Jesus when she was 12 years old. After graduating from Oak Harbor High School in northwest Ohio in 1980, she became a young wife and mother of three daughters.

Bonnie began her professional writing career at Hallmark Cards in their Christian division (DaySpring). She was promoted to Senior Writer after three years of employment. Her professional writing career has spanned 30 years. While employed at Hallmark, she began writing children's books through a partnership with HarperCollins Christian Publishing. Bonnie is the bestselling author behind the *Really Woolly* brand, with more than 1.6 million books sold, and the ECPA gold award-winning *Really Woolly Bedtime Prayers*.

Her three-book devotional series, *The Beach is Calling*, *The Campfire is Calling*, and *The Mountains are Calling*, consistently sells well and garners inspirational reviews, both publicly and through private messaging. *God in Every Moment* and *In This Together* are additional titles Bonnie has written for DaySpring. Publishers Bonnie has worked with include Barbour Publishing, DaySpring, Guideposts, Hachette Book Group, Hallmark, HarperCollins Christian Publishing, Paraclete Press, and Callisto Publishing.

ABOUT PARACLETE PRESS

Paraclete Press is the publishing arm of the Cape Cod Benedictine community, the Community of Jesus. Presenting a full expression of Christian belief and practice, we reflect the ecumenical charism of the Community and its dedication to sacred music, the fine arts, and the written word.

www.paracletepress.com

YOU MAY ALSO ENJOY . . .

CHRISTIAN POETRY IN AMERICA SINCE 1940

AN ANTHOLOGY

· EDITED BY ·

Micah Mattix and Sally Thomas

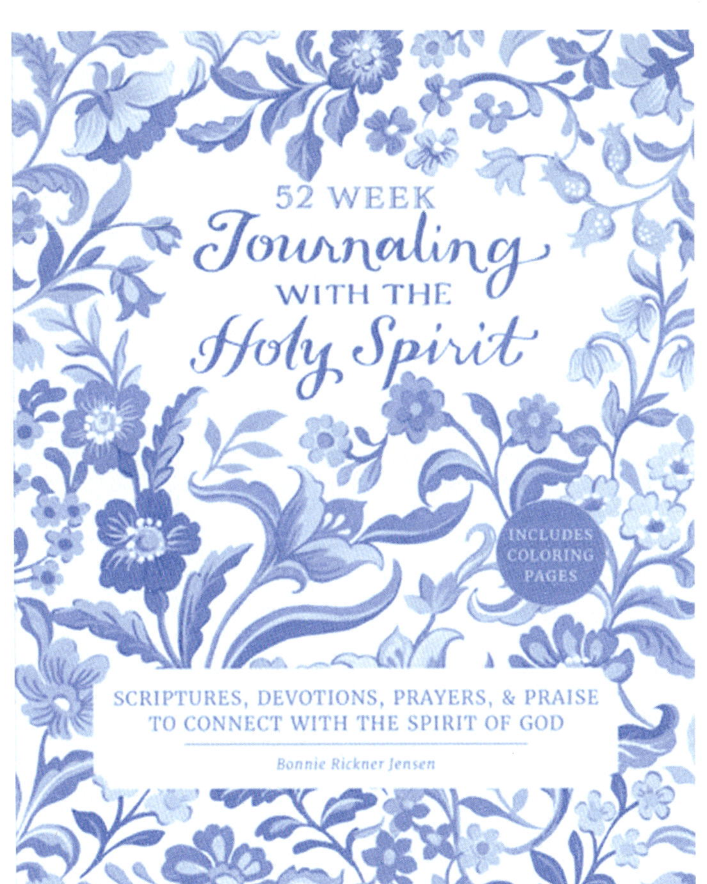
52 WEEK
Journaling
WITH THE
Holy Spirit
INCLUDES
COLORING
PAGES
SCRIPTURES, DEVOTIONS, PRAYERS, & PRAISE
TO CONNECT WITH THE SPIRIT OF GOD
Bonnie Rickner Jensen

IMAGE CREDITS

LOVE: William P. Chappel, *House Raising*, 1870s, Metropolitan Museum of Art.

PATRIOT: Archibald Willard, *The Spirit of 76*, 1912, City Hall, Cleveland, Ohio, USA.

FREEDOM: Emanuel Leutze, *Washington Crossing the Delaware*, 1851, Metropolitan Museum of Art.

PILGRIM: Jean Leon Gerome Ferris, *The First Thanksgiving*, 1621, United States Library of Congress.

HERITAGE: John C. McRae, *The Prayer at Valley Forge*, engraving after Henry Brueckner, 1866.

GLORY: Winslow Homer, *Home, Sweet Home*, 1863, National Gallery of Art.

DUTY: William B. T. Trego, *March to Valley Forge*, 1883, Museum of the American Revolution, Philadelphia.

RESILIENCE: George Washington at prayer, located in the Capitol Prayer Room, U.S. Capitol, Washington, D.C.

REPENTANCE: Albert Bierstadt, *Elk in Oak Grove (Tuolumne Meadows)*, circa 1875, property of the Townshend family.

COVENANT: Tablet on Lighthouse, Cape Henry, VA, 1896.

RIGHTS: Winslow Homer, *For to Be a Farmer's Boy*, 1887, The Art Institute of Chicago.

CONSTITUTION: U.S. Constitution, derivative image by Hidden Lemon.

HEALING: Winslow Homer, *An Afterglow*, 1883, Museum of Fine Arts Boston.

RISK: Eastman Johnson, *The Lord is My Shepherd*, 1863, Smithsonian American Art Museum.

LOYALTY: United States Library of Congress, Frederick Douglass, circa 1850—1860, modifications made by Chick Bowen.

MERCY: John Trumbull, *The Death of General Warren at the Battle of Bunker's Hill, 17 June, 1775*, 1786, Museum of Fine Arts, Boston.

BOLD: Currier and Ives, *Give Me Liberty or Give Me Death!*, 1876, Metropolitan Museum of Art.

REPUBLIC: John Trumbull, *Declaration of Independence*, 1819, United States Capitol Rotunda.

GENEROSITY: Winslow Homer, *Hudson River, Logging*, 1891/1892, National Gallery of Art.

HOPE: Edward Moran, *Unveiling The Statue of Liberty Enlightening the World*, 1886, Museum of the City of New York.

TRUST: Winslow Homer, *Fresh Eggs*, 1874, National Gallery of Art.

VISION: Edward Hicks, *Washington at the Delaware*, circa 1849, Chrysler Museum of Art.

ROSE: Winslow Homer, *Girl and Laurel*, 1879, Detroit Institute of Arts.

PROMISE: Harper's Weekly, *The first visit of William Penn to America*, 1883, Library of Congress.

STRENGTH: Harriet Tubman, circa 1871–1876, Library of Congress.

PROTECT: W. J. Bennett, *Three-Master American Barque*, 1830–1840, White House.

VICTORY: John Trumbull, *Surrender of Lord Cornwallis*, 1820, Rotunda of the U.S. Capitol.

UNITY: Letter Foundry of J. Howe & Co., *Specimen of Printing-Types, and Ornaments*, 1830.

PEACE: Albert Bierstadt, *Minnehaha Falls*, 19th century, Chrysler Museum of Art.

GRATITUDE: Winslow Homer, *The Whittling Boy*, 1873, Art Institute of Chicago.

TRANQUILITY: Henry Ossawa Tanner's image for *Harper's Young People*, 1893.

HOME: Thomas Cole, *Home in the Woods*, 1847, Reynolda House Museum of American Art.

(These public domain works of art are taken from Wikimedia Commons.)